New Habits

New Habits

TODAY'S WOMEN WHO CHOOSE
TO BECOME NUNS

ISABEL LOSADA

Hodder & Stoughton
LONDON SYDNEY AUCKLAND

British Library Cataloguing in Publication Data
A record for this book is available from the British Library

ISBN 0 340 72238 X

Typeset by Avon Dataset Ltd, Bidford-on-Avon, Warks

Printed and bound in Great Britain by
Clays Ltd, St Ives plc

Hodder and Stoughton Ltd
A Division of Hodder Headline PLC
338 Euston Road
London NW1 3BH

for Debbie
with love

contents

acknowledgements

Thanks to the ten inspiring women who wrote this book. Also thanks to: Mother Helen at All Saints for her patience; Mother Sheila and Sister Anne at Ditchingham for their time; Sister Rita Elizabeth at the Sisters of Bethany and Sister Gillian Mary at Tymayr for their encouragement and practical support; Sister Emma and Sister Mary-Jean at Tymayr for leaping with Joan; Sister Helena CHS, New York, for her energy; Joyce of CSF and Mother Christine from SJD for their faith in a stranger; Sister Winsome at Wantage who I'd like to have included; Dr Peta Dunstan: may all she does for ever prosper; Tony Edwards, a brilliant and sceptical scientist, for finding the book inspiring and for his continued faith in me; Lynne Schwahn and Jim Tieman for being there all that year; Linda Cowan for her gentleness; Helen Gummer for her prayers; Murray Watts who first suggested that I go on a retreat; Sister Anne-Julian at Wantage who first showed me the wisdom and love of the Sisters, and Sister Barbara-Thomas who thinks I've forgotten her; Roger Simpson, without whom life would have been very different; David Riley for his honesty; Phillip Whitehead MEP for telling me I can write, Anthony Minghella and Juliet Stevenson for their brilliance and compassion; Revd John Clarke for his smile; Sonya Leite, Menis Yousri, Ginny Fraser and Robert Razz for being my teachers; my daughter, Mez, for being my best and most patient teacher; Teresa Chris, my agent, for her humour; Judith Longman and Charles Nettleton at

Hodder for their commitment; Emma Mitchell, who took the photographs, for being a joy to work with; The Still Small Voice of Calm for love.

Introduction

How the Book Began

One of my dearest friends is going to become a nun. She is twenty-nine years old, very pretty, bubbly and huge fun to be with. She is a talented musician, plays six instruments and has so beautiful a singing voice that she is often asked to sing solo at weddings. She is a teacher, the kind of staff member who actually enjoys directing hundreds of children in a musical.

The religious community she seeks to enter is not a thriving group of women. My friend hopes to join a group of monks and two elderly women. No woman has entered this community and stayed in thirty years. Her first two applications were refused on the grounds that she was too young and needed more experience of life. Her third application, after much discussion, has resulted in a provisional acceptance for a trial period of six months.

She is a dangerous woman to ask to a party. Not that she talks about what she plans to do, but if someone should happen to ask if she is going to stay in teaching she will reply that she hopes to be a nun. The party comes to a halt. All conversation is, from this moment on, devoted to: 'You can't be serious!' 'You're going to be a nun???!!!' 'Will they lock you up?' 'Will you just pray all day?' 'Do you hate sex?'

'Haven't you ever had a lover?' 'But how do you know that God exists anyway?' 'But you're not Catholic.' 'But that is a waste of your life.' Then finally, when the outrage has died down, someone will ask: 'Why?' And the room will go quiet while my gentle friend explains her desire to pursue a spiritual life.

Everybody seems to be interested in nuns. A life with no pay, no sex either for fun or procreation, no chance to travel, no opportunity of promotion, nothing to strive for? Even simple pleasures like buying a piece of music, sleeping late, or wearing a new dress will be denied them. Yet they choose this lifestyle – no one has a gun to their heads. So I decided to speak to some more women who want to become nuns. What is in a convent that they will give their whole lives to experience? Can one really know God?

The Convent Visit

The first step was to visit a convent. I arranged a weekend with the Community of St Mary the Virgin at Wantage in Oxfordshire. I chose an Anglican community because no one seems to know that nuns and monks who are not Roman Catholic exist. I drove into the countryside on a Friday evening after work; it was snowing, there would be no other guests that night. I expected frigidity, an oppressive atmosphere of sexual suppression. I expected the nuns to be elderly, stooped, mainly in their eighties. I expected formality, a crucifix hanging on a bare wall. I expected a joyless silence. To be completely honest, I don't think I even expected the heating to work too well.

I arrived to be greeted by a smiling redhead aged about twenty-six (surely not another girl who is going to do this terrible thing?). I sat with the sisters at dinner humbled and amazed. They wore the traditional habits I had expected but they were dynamic, graceful and gracious. There were a handful of the stooped and elderly variety but the majority were in their thirties, forties and fifties. The community has over one hundred sisters and, most amazing of all, six novices – all younger than my own thirty-six years.

I had a wonderful weekend. It was joyful. There was a million times more joy in that place than in the television company I was working for at the time. There was laughter, peace and, most surprising of all, I could never have imagined what sensual places convents are. Leather sandals on marble floors, the chapel filled with old wooden pews, shiny with being polished. Warm sunlight through stained glass. The air filled with the scent of incense and fresh flowers everywhere.

There was a curious feeling of reality having been enhanced. I felt as if I was silently being shown how to be alive. It was as if there flowed from the sisters an excitement, an enthusiasm for each moment, a gratitude perhaps. In a television studio most of us are too busy trying to meet an impossible deadline to see the sun lighting the corner of a room or feel the skin of our own feet inside our shoes.

And there was no lack of humour at the convent. I saw a strange looking trapdoor and asked one of the novices, 'What's that?' 'Oh, that's where we smuggle men into the convent,' she said, roaring with laughter. I looked at her and said, 'I don't know why you are laughing. I can laugh – but if I was about to take a vow of celibacy for life, I don't know that I'd laugh quite so easily.' But this woman simply didn't have a problem with her choice.

An even greater surprise was that on Sunday afternoon I had no desire to leave and was already wondering when I could come back. There was a feeling of having arrived at last at a place that felt like home. How could I explain this? Could it have been the presence of love? Of all the prayer with which the sisters surrounded me? Or was there something more than both these? A strange feeling that Christ was right there, perhaps sitting in the next room, or closer still? I barely believed in God, yet I felt that I had spent the weekend in God's presence.

The Interviews

So I decided to give the women who wanted to 'waste their lives' a chance to speak. I had plenty of experience of interviewing for television, but I didn't want to use any format where I would come into the picture, either literally or metaphorically. So I simply took a tape recorder and let the novices talk. I asked all the questions I had heard my friend asked a hundred times at parties. I was fairly without mercy, not balking at the most difficult questions, either spiritually ('If there is a God of love then how do you account for innocent suffering?') or personal ('What happens to your sexuality in a place like this?'). And I transcribed what they said.

The Wisdom of Choosing

Misconceptions about nuns abound. The first is that only women who have been disappointed by love and are not able to get over it or are in denial of their sexuality could consider this as a life option. The idea that they are 'running away from life' prevails with the general public. The second is that convents and monasteries are desperate and would take anyone foolish enough to want to join them.

The reality is very different. First of all, many women who become nuns have had lovers or husbands before entering community, and even those who have not are forced to think through their attitudes to their sexuality far more than their friends left behind 'in the world'. The idea that to join a convent is 'to run away' is ironic as this is what the nuns are not able to do. In the secular world we have a thousand ways of avoiding our problems or our own thoughts. We may wake up to the radio, rush out to work, not have a moment all day for reflection, come home at night, perhaps watch television or read a newspaper before falling into bed. If we are troubled we can lift a telephone and talk to a friend. Many people are so unfamiliar with silence that the idea of spending an hour in silence in a room alone is frightening to them.

A woman who wishes to enter a convent will have none of these ways of avoiding her own thoughts. Imagine a world where, after nine thirty every evening, you will speak to no one until after breakfast the following day. Nor will you listen to a radio or switch on a television. In this situation it is necessary to learn rapidly to be at peace with yourself. No 'running away' is possible.

Those that can survive the discipline of this life are few. Many give up, many are advised to leave. On one of my first visits to a community I spoke to a guest who had lived with the sisters for two years and had dearly wanted to join them. The community had said that they felt the life was not for her and she had gone on to become a priest. She listened with amusement when I expressed my surprise at them 'turning away' a willing life member of the community.

The preparation to take life vows is long and hard, and I often think how many more marriages would survive if the process of making a life commitment to one partner was as rigorous. First, visits, as many as necessary. Then a commitment for six months, followed by the opportunity to make a promise of two or three years if all parties think it is a good idea. At the end of that period a chance to consider a promise for a further three to five years. Finally, after a trial period of seven years or more, comes the chance to promise to stay together for life.

One reason that convents are such joyful places is that everybody in them has chosen to be there – and has 'chosen the choice'. By this I mean they have gone further than simply choosing. They have chosen, and then considered and questioned the choice, and consciously taken the choice again. Very few people do this out here. How many spend their lives doing one job when they would really like to be doing another? They wake every morning without enthusiasm for the day ahead of them because they do not feel they have chosen their lives. Not so the nuns. They have taken free will with both hands and made a choice that they are encouraged to question until they are free of every vestige of uncertainty. They are where they believe they should be.

The Celibate Life

Personally I believe that the historical Church has done a huge disservice to the Creator by separating the sexual and the spiritual. Both these mysteries touch at the nature of our 'being'. If we could acknowledge that each person is a unique image of God then love, sexuality, deep respect and honour, one of another, could go together. The universal Church could be the first place to learn these things.

But of course the sisters would agree with me on this. It is not that they are against sexuality but it is just not compatible with the life. They choose to be 'wife and mother to none in order to be sister to all'. Sister Judith speaks beautifully of extending the love that some have for a partner – the care, the special attentiveness – to everyone around them. I have felt this when speaking to the sisters, especially the mothers of the communities. While I have been in their presence they give their whole being to attentiveness as if no one else in the world existed and I alone was of importance to them. To give that love we have inside us completely to all humanity is a high calling. I stand in admiration of all who are able to love in this way.

Aside from this, I can think of far worse ways to live. As the sisters have expressed, they always have a place to sleep, enough to eat and friends around them. Their companions share their ideas and have a common vision. They live lives where they are free to follow what they most love, which is to pursue their spiritual lives. They are 'free to be with God'.

Knowing God

There is plenty of spirituality around. The 'New Age' movement, with its thousand different viewpoints, has created, in North America and across Europe, a confusing collection of books in the section marked 'Mind, Body, Spirit'. They are mainstream and the readership is ever increasing. However, many of those who dedicate time, money and energy to their spiritual lives still find no peace in the silence of their own minds and hearts.

The depth of spirituality at the core of each interview is what the sisters have to share with the readers. I have asked each of the sisters how they know God, how they pray and how they believe that God speaks to them. Each sister has a different answer, a different perspective, a different experience – yet as the accounts deepen, a common thread of peace, silence and stillness becomes almost tangible through their words.

Teresa speaks of her whirlwind romance with God who, almost like a human lover, holds her or sits with her. Lynn speaks of the change in her thinking from conceptualising God as primarily outside herself to understanding God inside herself. Judith speaks of feeling herself one with all creation. Margaret looks for God in the most difficult moments of her work with homelessness, drug addiction and mental illness. Rachel says she is unafraid to use the worst language when expressing her anger to God. Helen sits in silence 'captivated by Christ'. Esther describes total fulfilment of her soul and being.

Meeting the Sisters

It is ironic that while there is widespread interest in nuns and monks there is also widespread ignorance of the Religious Life. More and more Roman Catholic nuns do not wear habits and so their ministry is becoming increasingly hidden. Outside the Roman Catholic Church, even members of the Anglican Church do not know that religious communities exist within their own communion. Whoopi Goldberg in *Sister Act* has now taken over from Julie Andrews in *The Sound of Music* as the dominant image of who a nun is. Yet peace of mind and heart is further and further from our reach.

Our convents and monasteries are powerhouses of the spiritually mature, vastly underused by those of us in the world who seek greater understanding of God and of ourselves.

I hope that listening to these women who have decided not just to visit a convent but to give their lives will overturn some of the myths. The honesty, candour and humour of these interviews made each of these women a joy to spend time with.

As you read, try and have a little stillness around you. If you can, turn off the radio, television and even the ever-intrusive telephone. Imagine a peace-filled silence. You sit in a room called 'Joy' – sparsely but comfortably furnished, a small table, wooden chairs, a view over a garden. A bell rings on the other side of a cloister. The door opens and there in front of you stands a nun. She wears a floor-length habit, a rope around her waist and the cross of her community around her neck. On her head is the white veil which tells you she is still a novice. Tea and biscuits are laid out on the table. She pours the tea, looks up, smiles . . . and starts to speak.

sister Teresa

My friends all thought it was quite natural that I should be becoming a nun. But there was one group of people who seemed totally amazed and that was those who went to my church. You would have thought that they would be happy to hear that I was going to dedicate my life to the God that they worship every Sunday, but they were all shocked and I remember one woman saying, 'What do you want to do that for?'

sister Teresa

SISTERS OF BETHANY

HAMPSHIRE, ENGLAND

Meeting Sister Teresa is a shock because she is, and looks, so young and so pretty that you think there must have been some mistake. Shouldn't she still be in school? The contrast is all the more extreme because the vast majority of her fellow sisters are of the traditional smiling and elderly kind which made me question whether this could possibly be the right place for her. Also the community is very traditional and I wondered if perhaps somewhere a little more modern would be better?
I was soon put in my place. Teresa is radiantly happy in her community and in many ways encourages them to be more traditional. Her honesty and almost raunchy sense of humour left me wondering whether the community would insist her interview was heavily edited, but they left it intact. Well, almost.

Sister Teresa is twenty-six and has been with the sisters for three years.

When I first visited the convent I had every intention of hating it. I thought I would see this bunch of miserable elderly nuns with their heads bowed saying the rosary. But people smiled and laughed and spoke to me and I couldn't hate it at all.

I didn't actually choose this community, it sort of landed on me. I woke up one morning, and I don't very often dream but this particular morning I knew what I had dreamt. I don't know if people want to call it a dream or a vision but I prefer to call it a dream, a powerful dream. Anyway, I saw myself in a habit. I had never thought at all about joining a religious community. I had never thought about being a nun and I thought all nuns were Roman Catholic.

I asked a friend what she saw me doing as a profession and she said she thought something caring, and when I told her that I'd had a dream that I was going to be a nun she said, 'Yes, that would suit you.' I rang my mum a week later and told her that I had come to a crossroads in life and didn't know which way to go next and she said, 'I know what you are going to do.' I was amazed and asked what. She said, 'You are going to join a convent.' She had never said anything about this and I asked her how she knew. She said, 'You told me when you were about eight years old and I always knew it would happen.' I had no recollection of this. On the strength of this call I decided perhaps I didn't need to go away and think, and went instead to see my priest to offer to become a Roman Catholic.

He explained that this wasn't necessary and I was given a list of Anglican communities to choose a couple to write to. I tried writing but tore up all my letters. The following day I went to a day of prayer at Guildford Cathedral. While I was waiting for the rest of my parish to arrive I saw a nun and went bounding after her and said, 'Er, excuse me, I think I want to be a nun.' And it was Sister Elvina from this community. She smiled and said she would meet me at lunchtime and that was how I came here.

The first day I came to the community, at just twenty-three, the window frames were painted green. They are cream now, but they were green and it was just like my grandad's house with green windows, and the gardens were beautiful and I felt as if I'd come home. In most Anglican communities twenty-five is the minimum age for taking life vows but this community does not have a minimum or maximum age for entry. I had my dream in February, met Sister Elvina in April and in October I arrived. I was twenty-three.

My father was a radiographer in the Army and my mother a nurse, and when I left school for the last time I counted ten schools that I'd been to. My brother and I lived in Hong Kong for three years, then Aldershot, then Germany, then Aldershot again, then we went to Cyprus for two years and then on to Hong Kong for another year. I certainly had plenty of experience of different cultures and we lived very much with the local people in Hong Kong and Cyprus. Eventually I ended up doing my O levels at a mixed comprehensive in North Yorkshire, when my dad left the army. I found the mixed comprehensive a bit of a shock after the encouragement and discipline of the military schools. In the military schools they are very tough and they push you and if you don't work hard they call you in and speak to you. At the comprehensive there was no discipline and I had a southern accent. At the first opportunity I left school and went straight to work. My first job was in a bank.

My home life was happy; we've always got on very well and I have very good relations with my mum and dad. My brother and I hated each other when we were younger of course, like typical siblings. I remember him stabbing my hand with a pencil, pretending it was an injection when we played doctors and nurses, and I still have the scar. And when we played hairdressers he cut all my hair off instead of pretending. A fairly typical big brother really.

When we arrived in a new country we usually visited the local church. We didn't go out of our way to find a church but if there was one on our doorstep we went, as long as we liked the vicar. If we didn't like the vicar we didn't go. My parents don't go to church now.

I was in a church choir when I was eleven because I liked singing; I got confirmed. The only reason I got confirmed was because I wanted to have the wine and the bread like everyone else. It didn't mean anything. I was eleven years old. And after my confirmation I hardly went to church at all between the ages of twelve and twenty-two. My mum says I was always a goody-goody and now I'm a professional goody-goody.

When I was twenty-two I drove past a church that I'd been to as a child, so I got out to have a look at it. I met a churchwarden there who remembered our family and was very friendly and invited me to go in and look around. It is a High Anglican church and they use a good pile of incense. When I went in, the smell of it brought the joy of church back to me and I went to visit on the Sunday morning. I'd only been going just short of a year when I got 'the call'!

But I haven't told you what happened after the bank when I was sixteen. I managed to survive there for three years, but when I was nineteen I travelled across Canada and that was enough to show me that I was certainly ready to leave the bank. I moved out of home when I was twenty and I got my own flat. I did temping for a while and worked as a nanny, I had a job as an office administrator, and worked in a delivery company as their administrator. I worked in a hotel for a year and then I moved down south and worked for a computer distribution company. The job with computer distribution had all sorts of perks. I won hundreds of vouchers and once the department won a trip to Euro Disney and we had a wonderfully drunken weekend. I had just been offered a new job with the salary I'd asked for when I left to come to community. I think it would be true to say that I had a wide experience of different types of work.

And I did notice boys when I was growing up. I started early with boyfriends when I was ten and had loads of boyfriends until I was thirteen. Between thirteen and seventeen I didn't really have any proper boyfriends and I used to worry and try really hard. I was interested in all the movie stars, the pop singers, the heroes at school, but although I was always interested in them I didn't do well during those years. Friends said I had a barrier up and I complained, 'But I want a man and I want to experience love.' I feel now that maybe I was protected from the free sex environment that was happening around me.

When I was seventeen I fell in love with a wonderful man. My heart jumped the first time I saw him. He asked me out to dinner and we started dating. He was terribly romantic. He used to open doors for me and send me flowers every week. He took me out for a meal every week and he taught me how to shoot tin cans and clay pigeons and we went swimming. We had a wonderful six months and he put no demands on me at all. Anyway I broke it off after that because I realised he was getting very serious and I didn't feel ready to make a serious commitment to him. I found out after I broke it off that he had bought me a ring so I know I was right that he was getting serious. He still sent me flowers even after we broke it off. There is a lot more to the story but that is all you are getting!

The months between the dream and arriving here were not easy ones. As I said, I'd just been offered a new job and I wasn't sure whether I should take it. My father was seriously ill at the time and, although thankfully he has recovered now, I wasn't sure whether I should go home and help look after him. And although my parents were happy about my coming here, some of the family didn't feel it was necessarily the right choice for me. There was the usual thought that I was 'running away from life' to go to a convent. Of course what people don't realise is that when you go to a convent you 'run' slap bang into yourself.

Actually there was nothing I was running away from. I'd just been offered the job I wanted at the salary I wanted. And I suppose those who were not in touch with me thought that I must be thinking 'I'm still on the shelf (at twenty-three!): obviously no one is ever going to love me, so I'll join a convent instead.' But that simply wasn't true. The friends that were around me at the time were not surprised when I told them – which surprised me. I was expecting them to say 'What? You're joking!' but they actually said 'Oh, good!'

I would say that I was called, but what that means to me is that I was led here, drawn here, in the way that I've described to you.

Someone who came here at the same time as me said, 'It was like watching a whirlwind romance, watching your calling.' And that was what it felt like. Sometimes I thought it was happening too fast, but at other times I didn't feel it was happening fast enough. I didn't feel that I needed to travel and see the world before I came in because I spent my entire childhood living in different cultures.

Having a whirlwind romance with God is breathtaking. I was not having visions every day and I did not get on my knees and pray for five hours at a time or anything as dramatic as that. I am not a saint by any means. But it was a feeling of knowing that some 'thing' (in order not to put God into a human sense), was holding me in his arms. The times that I felt, 'This is happening too fast', he was holding me. The times that I felt it was not happening quickly enough he was sitting there waiting with me. I can't describe what the emotion is – it's joy, it's wonderful. I still feel that I'm in a whirlwind, it hasn't gone. No doubt it will, sometime. If I take my vows it will probably go then and hit me like a ton of bricks, and I'll think 'What have I done?' But I don't think so. It's so 'me'. I feel so free to be myself here.

However, it hasn't been all plain sailing. Just over a year ago, when I had been here two years, things were not going well. I felt that I was in the wrong community. I thought that maybe I was being called to a contemplative community. I told the Mother here that I thought maybe I should visit one. I went for a weekend and felt totally elevated and I came back thinking, 'This is the place.' I asked if I could go for a month and shortly after that I rang here and confirmed that I would be joining the contemplatives. A date was fixed for me to enter the new community, I came back and had my habit removed and went back home to visit my parents for five weeks. They decided that we should all go to Malta on a holiday. While we were away something – no words, no vision, but something – told me it was wrong. I came back from the holiday and wrote to both communities. I wrote to the one I was supposed to be joining and told them that I would not be coming after all. I wrote to this community to let them know of my decision, as I had not left here under a cloud or anything.

I made up my mind I definitely wasn't going to enter any community ever again. I got a job and I started looking for a house to buy and everything was going fine, but for this feeling that there was something missing. One day the phone rang and it was the Reverend Mother from here just making a friendly phone call to ask how I was, had I got a job, etc. That was all it was – we were on the phone five minutes. I was pleased to hear that everyone was all right. Then gradually I had this growing knowledge that I wanted to go back. I thought I must be crazy.

Anyone that joins a community is nuts. What woman do you know that would want to live with a bunch of twenty women that have weird habits and dress funny? It's not natural. No one in their right mind would join a community. And I had made up my mind that there was no way I was ever going back. But the feeling didn't go away. One morning I ended up in tears before work and said to Mum and Dad, 'I'm sorry, I want to go back into community.' They were fine. I rang up Mother and asked if I could come and see her and asked if I could come back. I had to think about why I left though.

Basically I still feel called to be a contemplative, but I can't go into an enclosed community. I wouldn't do that to my family. At the moment, my grandparents live nearby and I can visit them once a month. I love seeing my grandparents and I think they enjoy seeing me even more. My parents can come down and take me out for the day every three months or so and I have four weeks' 'rest' a year that I can spend wherever I want. Also my brother, who is hopeless at planning anything in advance, can just ring up at nine o'clock in the morning and say, 'I'm arriving at two, is that all right?' and they'll say 'Yes'. Then he'll end up arriving at four – but we still love him!

In the strict enclosed life I was considering I would have had one visit for an afternoon every three months and two weeks' rest. If I didn't have family I would go into an enclosed community. But having said that, I wouldn't be in this community if I didn't think God wanted me here. If I really felt God wanted me in an enclosed community I would go. When the work is prayer, from my understanding, the more in depth your prayer life is the fewer distractions you want. Family and friends are great but they can be a major distraction from your focus. I find letters about 'Ann Summers' parties amusing and when friends ask if I'd like a Jackie Collins book sent in brown paper I smile. But in an enclosed community it just isn't the same. You want to concentrate wholeheartedly on God and you just don't want distractions like that. There is a depth of prayer you are seeking there and you don't want visitors all the time.

Our community is called the 'Sisters of Bethany' after the sisters Mary and Martha that Jesus visits in Bethany. In the story, Mary is a contemplative and sits at the feet of Jesus and Martha does the work and serves the tables. We all have some Mary and some Martha in us. This community allows people to be Marthas and/or Marys. I now feel that what God was showing me through all this is that I am a Mary but I need my Martha near me. In fact I am a Sister of Bethany.

I do not feel the presence of God twenty-four hours a day. It is a knowledge that he is there. I sometimes feel like changing the first line of the Creed which goes, 'I believe in one God'. I feel that it suggests doubt and that we could possibly be wrong. I want to change it to 'I know there is one God'. I don't feel his presence all the time but I know he's there. I know there is air. I can't see it and I can't always feel it but I know it is there because I'm breathing it.

It is a knowledge that you can't back up with logic. My prayer life is erratic and I don't always have a wonderful experience every time I pray, but I do have a prayer life. I was asked when I first came into community to write something on what I thought about prayer. My way of describing prayer is that it is communication with God. It isn't always a two-way conversation. Sometimes I listen to God and most of the time I don't. He always has the receiver up. He is always ready to listen to me. When I pray, it is the time when I hope I listen to him. I pray twenty-four hours a day because I'm living for God, living with God. My specific times of meditation are my quality one-to-one times with God. I aim to think nothing but God. But my concentration is still pretty hopeless and if I hear a noise I will look to see where it has come from.

When I first came here I had two half-hour sessions of meditation a day and I was lucky if I could keep still for a minute – and as for trying to concentrate for a half an hour, it was an absolute impossibility. I now get up earlier than I have to in order to get one hour's prayer in. If someone had told me even two years ago that I would have been doing one hour's prayer in the morning I'd have said, 'Get away! I'd never do that.' I'm finding I'm more comfortable with the one-to-one relationship with God. I still get angry with God and I have been known to throw a slipper in the direction of the crucifix when I'm in my room. I use the worst unrepeatable language with God sometimes, but if you love someone you feel free to show all your emotions with them. I feel he should intervene more often. Far more often.

I use different forms of prayer. Sometimes I use a mantra, which is a verse or a word that you keep repeating all the time. For example 'Alleluia' which means 'Praise the Lord'. I also use the Orthodox rosary and the Catholic rosary, but most of the time I just sit. There is a proverb from 5000 BC that says 'The way to do is to be'. And this is what I'm learning – it is enough just to be there for God. I don't try to do anything or even be anything. And if a thought comes I just let it float away. I'm just being, like a tree is just being. I don't get a wonderful sensation every time – in fact it very rarely happens, but when it does it reaffirms my beliefs. It is difficult to describe one of these special times. It's a bit like lying on a gigantic bean bag and you can make it comfortable in every position you want.

I can remember one period when I wanted to know the answers to everything. Would I stay here? Would I be professed? What would happen? When would I die? What happens after you die? What's going to happen to my family? I wanted to know everything all at once. I remember being in chapel – I don't know how long I was in there. And I felt like I was in the desert surrounded by a huge sand dune that was all around me. On the other side of the sand dune were all the answers, but I knew that no matter how much I tried I was going to slip back down. And it made me realise that I'm not going to get all the answers. I'm not going to know everything now. I may learn some of the answers, but I'm not going to know everything in this life. It was a beautiful way of being told the answer. I'm not sure if it was a picture or an emotion, I'm not sure if I saw the sand dune or felt it. But I know it was there. And I know there was something magnificent on the other side. And I couldn't get there. And it was beautiful.

I have never heard a voice. God does not speak to me over a Tannoy system. I feel God speaks to me through emotions and feelings. I like to have a good cry, I do get angry and I like to let off steam, but I don't tend to do it in the presence of people. I can usually hold things till I can be alone with God. God speaks to me through my gut and through the working out of things. This doesn't make any sense, does it? I let things bottle up, and when I let the cork out I let God in and let the things come out. This is really difficult.

I tell you what drives me crazy here and that is when we recite the psalms and someone is out of time. I like it when we are all together, but when someone is too fast or too slow nothing is ever said. Gone are the days when in community if there was a sister who was tone deaf she would be politely asked not to sing. Now everyone sings and everyone speaks and if anyone is out of time it is too bad. But how beautiful it sounds when everything goes right!

If I could change anything I would introduce the use of far more incense. People have been offering it to God for thousands of years, way back into the Old Testament. I find it a very powerful form of prayer and why stop doing it? But you accept that everyone's churchmanship is different. Here we only use incense on very big feasts.

Poverty, Chastity and Obedience

Poverty. I don't find material poverty a problem. I don't have my own car any more but there is a car here I can borrow if I need to go anywhere. I don't spend loads of money on clothes any more, but then I don't need them. I don't spend £100 on jewellery any more because I don't need it. And the poverty here is relative. Although we own nothing, we have everything we need.

I don't miss anything. In some sense it's the same as marriage, isn't it? When you marry someone you give up your own home and move in with that person and give up your total independence. You centre your whole being around your new partner. So although I have given up a lot I don't feel as if I've given up a lot, because I've changed my life.

There is huge joy in giving things away. I had my grandmother's engagement ring for years. Just as I was coming here I discovered that my sister-in-law had lost her engagement ring. With my dad's permission I gave her this engagement ring. I've given clothes to my friends. It was as much a joy giving my possessions away as it was receiving them in the first place.

There is no possessiveness here, it is not my work or my book or even my room – it is the community's. It is our book, our work.

Then there is spiritual poverty, but I don't think I can explain that. Ask me in ten years. What did the others say?

★ ★ ★

Chastity. Here we vow chastity, not celibacy. It is keeping yourself purely focused on God. Not reading the Jackie Collins book or going to the Ann Summers party. When you are married you keep yourself focused on your husband or wife. It is not a good thing if you are married to your husband and spend your whole time drooling over your next-door neighbour. This is not a good thing for marriage. Likewise it's not good to keep your mind focused on your husband or wife but have sex with your next-door neighbour. In chastity we are keeping our body and our mind clear for God. It is more than celibacy. So no Jackie Collins books. Shame, I like Jackie Collins. Er, liked Jackie Collins.

I am very happy to join the community being the traditional virgin. I did have serious boyfriends after the legal age of sex, but although the relationships were physical ones they never went as far as intercourse, although we got pretty close sometimes. I was very much in love and I had a wonderful relationship. The fact that we never made love does not mean that I didn't get aroused. I mean, I'm still a woman and I'm not afraid of my sexuality.

For me, I'm glad I have come in as a virgin but I don't really know why. I enjoy offering the fact that I'm a woman to God. Because I focus on God and not on the men that walk past. I mean, I still notice if I see an attractive man and I think 'Oh yes!' – and that still happens, but it is not to the extreme that I feel I want to take my habit off and run away with this man. It is appreciating that God made this person and he is attractive. Alleluia! In a similar way that a woman may look at another woman and think, 'What a wonderful figure!' The Lord made her with a figure that women would die for. But I don't look at men any more and think, 'I wonder how I can get him?' That is not how I look at them, and I'm not saying that I don't see one and think 'Wow, he's nice!' But it doesn't go any further. Not because I'm 'suppressing' it. I just don't act on it. I get double-takes when I go out in a habit. I think it's because I'm so young. My mum loves walking down the street with me because people look at me, and any excuse to talk to me they'll take and my mum says they are probably thinking, 'But she's pretty, why is she in a habit?' But I just don't have any desire to leave here.

I've been told that if you are in tune with your sexuality you can read the Song of Solomon without blushing. I think that is an amusing test and I don't ever have any trouble reading it in chapel. I don't try and hide my sexuality, or all that being a woman means. I am a young woman with boobs, periods and feelings. I can appreciate someone who is good-looking, but I don't have a desire to sleep with anyone. And that is a relief because, before, I was trying to fit into a stereotype of standing at the pub with my friends, thinking, 'Yes, he's nice. No, he's not nice.' I was trying to fit into a type that I'm not. I suppose if I felt 'Yes I've got to get that man', I couldn't be here.

The world goes on and on that I am missing the most important experience. But at the risk of sounding absurd, I've got God. Some people feel fulfilled in their job. Some people, if they are Christians, feel that going to church once a week and sending up prayers like arrows during the day is going to fulfil their life. I don't feel as if I'm missing out here. I feel that I'm gaining and giving more than I ever did before.

I went through a stage where I was very broody, age about eighteen to twenty-one, and I was desperate for a man to come along so I could have babies. But in reality, although my mother and my grandmother would disagree, I don't feel that I would make a very good mother. My mother says that the only thing she feels is sad about my being in community is that I won't be a mother. But having children is a vocation in itself and I don't feel it is my vocation.

It is important to say that there is actually no padlock on the door and no wall around the convent. If I did feel differently in my late thirties, there is no electric fence to stop me leaving. It is the equivalent of a divorce and about as difficult where paperwork and emotional upheaval is concerned.

People say that it is an 'unnatural life' and I totally agree. It is far more normal to get married and have children. So? God calls people to all walks of life. I mean Jesus never married. There are the accusations that he was gay or that he was married to Mary Magdalene, but in the Bible he never married. He lived a life of celibacy, obedience to his father God and a life of poverty. He said that he had nowhere to lay his head. But 99.9 per cent of people are called to the 'Adam and Eve' life, where man is made for woman and woman is made for man. But I'm very happy in this life.

★ ★ ★

Obedience. This is the hardest one for me. Obedience to God through the community. For someone my age … When I was working, I was fighting all the time to be treated as an adult and to have my own mind and be appreciated for having one. When you come in to community at my age, bang, you are a child again. You are not in a position to argue with anyone. If someone asks you to do something you say 'Yes Sister' and you do it, even if it seems absurd. You see someone doing something in a way that is completely wrong, and you see that you are wasting time and energy but in obedience you accept that they have asked you to do it this way. I mean, tea towels! This is a perfect example from the laundry: with a tea towel, you wash it. And when you pull it out and it's wet you iron it, with your hands. You spend ages flattening it out with your hands and then you hang it out and you don't need to iron it. In my mind you could dry it as it was and then give it a quick iron. It would be a lot quicker and easier. But they have always done it that way, so I do it that way. And that is the way of obedience! They'll kill me for saying that.

Another one, the pantry. We have a dishwasher and before we put the plates in the dishwasher, we wash them, and then afterwards we dry them. Why do you need to dry them? Because if you leave them for just a few minutes, they'll get dried on their own. God will dry them! But no – it's community. So we dry them.

So, as you see, for me it is not obedience in the big things that bothers me but only the little ones, and every now and again I have to go down to the woods and scream. It's full of these things. This particular community can be very old-fashioned but they have come on an awful lot even since I've joined. Changes are being made all the time.

There are some parts of the tradition that I'm glad they've kept. Like standing up when the Reverend Mother comes in. That is a lovely mark of respect. And they stand up when a visitor comes in or leaves the room as a sign of humility and to give that person respect. Can you imagine a society where people genuinely showed one another that level of respect? There is something very moving about a woman of eighty standing up because a visitor comes in to the room.

As regarding obedience in larger matters, there is a clause in our Rule which says that if you feel that you have been asked to do something that you do not feel called to do, you can approach the senior and say why you don't feel God is calling you to do it. She would then say, 'We'll look at it again.' If she said, 'I'm sorry but this is what we want you to do', under obedience, I'd do it.

I can relax and be me here so fully. And I can have time with God. Before I came into community I tried desperately to have a disciplined spiritual life. I didn't. I have very little self-discipline. In one way, if you want to be a committed Christian and committed to your spirituality it is a very easy option. You have the timetable around you. You have the help and the discipline around you. You never have to worry about when and where to pray. I don't have to worry about the work. I don't have to make sixty outgoing phone calls a day. If I don't finish the work I have to do today, it doesn't matter, I can do it tomorrow. If I get way behind, someone will help me. People help each other. If you are ill they look after you. If you have joyous news it is news they all enjoy. If my family come to visit, the whole community is excited because their family has come to visit. It's not just my mum and dad, it's everyone's mum and dad. It's not just my brother, it's everyone's brother. We don't just share possessions, we share our lives. When my family go away they send a card to all of us. And because the sisters have accepted my family so much, my family can accept them.

They don't judge you at all. They don't care if you get spots, or are as fat as an elephant. They embrace you. So what if a sister likes to pour coffee on her cereal? Outside people may think 'Yeuk' but if that is her way, let her be. You accept that everyone has funny ways. Not only do they wear a habit, but they may have irritating habits as well. But here it doesn't matter if a sister picks her nails. There is a freedom to be you.

You don't have the worries of fashion, job, money or work, so you can free yourself to be with God and pray on behalf of those people that do have that worry and offer them up to God. And you are free to be with God all the time.

Since this interview Sister Teresa has taken her life vows. She writes:

'The service was beautiful, all my family attended – and I know it was not easy for them, but I know they enjoyed the day.

'At the end of the service we have a sung response which is a very moving piece of music, I sang with my sisters responding; my first line started "He is my beloved, and he is my friend . . ." I always have been His and I always will be.

'I belong to Christ. What more can I say?'

sister rachel

One of my friends said, 'You can still get married and be normal and have kids and serve God, you know. You don't have to become a nun for goodness sake!'

sister rachel

Arriving at this community you travel to the heart of Birmingham's Asian community. The old convent has had to sell almost all of its grounds over the years with the result that it now feels a little squashed. I had the impression that there is no money to spare here. The sisters, despite being mainly elderly, are in normal clothes and very informal.

As I'm visiting they decide to abandon the silent lunch to chat about my book. The food was like school lunches with jam pudding and custard for dessert. Some of the sisters remind me of storybook grandmothers, always happy, healthy and smiling. They obviously all adore their newest novice and are very proud of her. I found myself wishing that Rachel was not the only sister in her twenties, but they had an enthusiasm and an energy which somehow belied their age.

I was invited to join them in the traditional chapel for midday prayers. A large crucifix with Christ, not resurrected, but for ever on his cross, takes the

central position over the altar but the reading for the day, about the
need to forgive those that have hurt us, could have been a reply to the
headlines of the morning's papers. I was very touched that, although I
had only arrived that day, my life and family and the progress of
this book were all included in the prayers.

Sister Rachel is twenty-nine and has been in the Community for a year.

I thought I'd be in the middle of the countryside in a beautiful Olde Convent with a huge garden and cloisters and everyone wearing a habit. And look at where I am – I'm in the middle of a run-down area of inner-city Birmingham, we certainly don't have cloisters and we wear our own clothes.

The community was founded in 1848 by a bishop and a doctor who were concerned about poor nursing standards. The sisters started training nurses. Some of them went to the Crimea with Florence Nightingale and the 'Mother's cross', which Christine now wears, went to the Crimea. In the 1930s the sisters started taking vows and it became more specifically a religious community. They were involved in midwifery and nursing in the East End of London and they had a nursing home at Hastings. In the early 1970s a group of sisters went to Malawi to set up a midwifery training school, and in 1976 the community's main house came to Birmingham. At the moment all the sisters here are trained nurses but you no longer have to be a trained nurse to join the community. The ethos of this community is health, healing and reconciliation.

The only mystically spiritual experience I had as a child was when I was about five, and I remember it quite clearly: My mum had been washing my brother and me in the bath and my mum had lifted my brother out, and I can remember having a sudden feeling of how big the world was and how small I was – like God touching me in some way. I can't explain but it was a feeling of being validated for being me in this great big enormous world. A feeling of who I was.

My mother was a missionary in Botswana and my father was a geologist in the overseas service. My brother and I were born in South Africa. When we came back to England, I was plunged straight into school, which I think was a bit of a shock as I'd been left fairly much to my own devices in Africa. Also my mother was ill at this time and my younger brother and I were sent off for a while to live with my aunt and uncle. It was a difficult time for us all settling back into England.

We moved to a small village outside Cambridge, which is where I did most of my growing up. I went to the village primary school and then to the local mixed comprehensive school, which I didn't like. It was large and rough and I didn't make friends easily. I was full of angst and a typically traumatised teenager. I was not encouraged to join the disco, party, boyfriend scene, and I wasn't particularly gregarious at that age. I was never very settled there, but I stayed until my O levels and then did A levels before going to Keele University to do Greek and Roman Studies. I did the parties and clubs scene at university with all the other students. We went out to the Union and got back at two in the morning and slept till eleven – and I had loads of friends there. It was a very normal student life, I suppose. Then, when I left university, I started my training to become a nurse.

To go back a bit. As we were growing up, we were always very involved with the life of the church. It was quite 'High Church', which wasn't my mother's background at all. I can remember once there was a notice on one of the chapels which said, 'The blessed sacrament is reserved'. I said to my mum, 'What does that mean?' and she said, 'It means you have to be quiet.' She was the daughter of a minister in the United Reformed Church, and when I was between six and eight, she used to go to Quaker meetings and I went with her sometimes. I remember just sitting with her, in the silence And I think that made quite an impression on me. As a teenager I worried a lot about whether God existed or not, and I felt there was nothing to prove it. When I was fifteen, I was confirmed. I was very confident and determined that I wanted to be confirmed. It was very much something that I wanted to do, not something that I was pushed into. In fact, if anything, I was discouraged from being confirmed before I was ready. I grew a lot through that and having to take responsibility for my own faith, rather than it being something that I did because of my parents' faith.

From the age of about fourteen, I thought I might have a vocation to be a nun but I kept very quiet about it, and I remember in my final year at university seeing a baby in a pram and thinking, 'I don't want to do this thing about having a vocation because I want to get married and have a family.' For a while I dropped out of church completely because I felt that going to church meant that I had to test my vocation. So I gave up on my faith. For nearly a year I enjoyed lying in bed on a Sunday morning. But having made a very rational decision not to be a Christian any more, I actually found that God did not just go away because I told him to go away. I've always had a lot of uncertainties and doubts about my faith and I thought that, if I gave it all up, I could commit myself to the doubt, to live feeling that there was no God. I needed to let go of the belief that had been given to me by my family and find what was left – and this was a good experience. I fear I never managed to fully embrace atheism and only really got as far as agnosticism. I really wanted to get out of my vocation.

I came to Birmingham after my degree, and at twenty-two started work and living and working at a residential centre with the mentally ill – mainly schizophrenic and people who had been in mental institutions most of their lives. I made some very good friends in that time and I was more sort of 'in touch' with people's suffering than I had been.

I was beginning to think about my faith again. I'd said to God, 'If you want me to test my vocation, you've got to do something about it because I just don't know what you want me to do.' One Tuesday I got up to go shopping and realised that I wanted to go to communion at Birmingham Cathedral. I got there and the vicar said, 'Today is the feast day of St Anthony of the desert, one of the monastic saints, so we are praying for vocations to religious communities. I have invited

Sister Dorien, from our own community of St John the Divine, to administer communion.' And I thought, 'Oh no!! I think I'm going to have to say something to this nun!' So, as we were all going out, I said, 'Er, could I have a word with you? I think God may be calling me to join a community.' That was how I first came to visit.

I moved to the nurses' home and lived there for three years while I trained, and then came to live with the community for six months, so I could share the life while I looked for a job. I was twenty-six by this time. Then I moved out and got my own flat in Birmingham for two years while I worked in an adolescent psychiatric unit. I also worked for a while in a private psychiatric clinic, which was valuable because I saw a wider range of problems. When I was twenty-eight I came here.

I think I was 'called'. I think we are all called to live our life in a certain way and that within that there are specific callings. I think I'm called to this way of life and that's why I'm here. In my mid teens I wondered if I should be ordained, but the sense of being called to be a sister was greater. It was a kind of picture and a strong feeling that that was what I was meant to be doing.

I remember two instances where I remember being very aware of what it would mean. I remember a husband and wife that I knew. The wife was ill, and I remember the husband looking at her with real love and concern and care for that one other person. It was two people who had given themselves to each other and I was very aware that, if I was to be a sister, I would never experience that kind of love. Secondly, I watched a friend of our family with his small son. He bent over his son to give him a kiss on the top of the head and there was a beautiful feeling of the love of parent for child and I knew that, if I was a sister, that was another thing I would not experience. And these feelings were very strong.

As I became aware of the Religious Life and the kind of a life that was there, there was something in me that said, 'This is what I am meant to be doing.' A response from inside myself – I can't put it into better words than that.

I don't think faith is about intellectual processes. It is about a response to something outside us and inside us and sometimes you have to let go of the intellectual nitty gritty like, 'Well, where are you exactly, God? And what are you?' and let God touch you. Sometimes God has touched me, and I've felt very aware of him and very aware of his presence and of him working within me. These times are not often, and there isn't a lot and I can't put it into words; it's just a feeling, an awareness. When I used to go to the Quakers, I can remember sitting there and being silent and being very aware that the door was open; and I could see out of the door and there was a garden and at that age I didn't think, 'God is here', but I was aware of something beyond me.

It is very hard to describe the feeling of God's presence. I don't want to say something that just sounds like a cliché . . . It is easy to say, 'I feel peace' or 'I feel joy' and yet sometimes that is what it feels like – you feel peaceful, joyful or fulfilled. I remember, before I came to the community, I came on a retreat here for about five days and every day I used to go and walk around the park here and there was a feeling of rightness, being centred, things being in their place, and being in tune with myself and with God. That was at the point when I was seriously beginning to move towards coming here, so these feelings of it just being right and feeling at peace about the decision were one way I discerned the way forward.

My decision to go into nursing had been based on an attempt to integrate what I believed and felt into my life. I wanted to nurse because I had a faith, and I thought it was important to do something in which the values I held in my life could be shown in what I did. Also, before coming here, I became an associate of this community which involved having a rule of life with a commitment to prayer, spiritual reading and the work of reconciliation.

My training as a nurse influenced the way I see my faith and the way

I see my calling as a Christian. I can remember quite early on in my training I was looking after a child who had been abused, physically abused, and she used to scream herself to sleep when she was put into bed. She was about two years old. I can remember taking her in my arms because she would sleep if you held her. I think I read her a story sitting on the side of the bed and she dropped off to sleep; and I sat with this child and started praying for her. I just prayed for her, I gave her to God, because you wonder what life held for her. That was a moment when I felt very close to God. It felt as though he was right there. That encapsulates what I feel I'm meant to be doing. It is just being there alongside people and sometimes all you can do is pray for them. There is a kind of helplessness because when you see how much unhappiness and suffering there is, you can feel overwhelmed and horrified by it.

When I made the decision to ask to become a novice, I had been a postulant but I knew I had to make a definite decision about whether I wanted to stay; I just didn't know. They said, 'You will know', and I didn't believe them because I felt my experience was that God had never spoken to me that clearly. How could I possibly be sure of what was right for me? And it was March and the children were massacred in Dunblane. I remember watching that on the news in the evening; I couldn't even watch all the news. I went and sat at the back of chapel. I remember saying to God, 'Well I'm here, I really don't know what to say. I want to pray but I can't. It just seems so utterly awful and all I can do is be here.' I didn't hear a voice but I knew that, if I said 'No' and didn't come here, it would be like saying 'No' to those children. I couldn't say 'No' to being there, to just being alongside people, either physically in body or just by praying for them, and I had to say 'Yes'.

I've chosen to live a life which is based on prayer and it is very demanding. There is no measurement. No one arrives and says, 'Ah Rachel, you are there now. You are living a life of prayer!' I think for all Christians prayer has to be the basis, the cornerstone of their spiritual life. One of the things I do is to spend time in the early morning in chapel and I think about the day. In the evening I pray more for others and for all the people who have asked for my prayers. I don't mince words with God. Sometimes I'll storm around my room and say, 'Come on, God, what's going on here? Get your act together! I'm going to murder Sister So-and-so soon. Oh, you'd better not write that or she'll know who it is! Where was I? Oh yes, shouting at God. Well, the result of this is that I start to work through the problems instead of running away from them. Tomorrow may be a bad day and I may write to you and say: 'Don't listen to what I said.' The thing about community is that you can't run away from your problems. You have to work through them. The only way to run away is to leave, and then you are running away from yourself and can only take the problems with you. Prayer is part of my growth as a person. If you think God wants you here, you have got to face the things in community that are difficult. As a result of prayer you have to be prepared to make yourself vulnerable and to go out and meet what's coming your way and to deal with it. You can say that happens in anybody's growth, whether they are a believer and praying or not, but in my case I am aware of ways in which prayer has helped me. I sit down and say, 'Well, what are we going to do about this?'

I often tell God exactly what I think he should be doing. Whether he does what I tell him or whether he does it in the way I want him to is another matter, but it doesn't stop me telling him.

Also, I respond to beauty; and quite often I'll go out, just to walk, and I'll feel the wind in my hair or I'll just wander round the garden. This is a very informal version of prayer with no words, and I just become aware of myself and of God being around me and in me and with me. It doesn't take words; it just happens.

Over the time when I first came here, I was looking at different kinds of ministries and different kinds of work that I might want to become involved with in the community in the future. Although I don't think that I want to nurse for good, my nursing has made me very aware of the idea of wholeness and wholeness of people, emotional and physical. I think where my ministry lies is to try and help people on the journey towards wholeness as people have helped me to grow. I'd like to think that I'll be involved in the pastoral care of people. Because of that I am doing a pastoral studies (counselling) diploma at Westhill College in Birmingham. They are mostly just active churchgoers and perhaps the odd priest, but I'm the only sister. I didn't go to the first session, and they heard that there was going to be a nun amongst them so they were all expecting an elderly penguin.

As well as this, I'll be helping in the local parishes, and I also hope to be involved with the Asian, and particularly the Muslim women that live locally. We, as a community, need to respond to the people who are around us. We need to – well, I need to. I feel that it is right for me to go out and learn from and be involved with the local community. We are in quite a deprived area and there is a whole other culture here that I would like to be meeting and mixing with.

Poverty, Celibacy and Obedience

I haven't actually taken vows yet because I have only been clothed as a novice. That simply means that you live with the community and try to live the life that you would live when you take vows. So the fact that you haven't taken vows does not mean that you can pop out and say, 'I think I'll have a quickie tonight', because you'd have to ask yourself, 'Well, if I can't manage it now, am I going to be able to manage it when I'm in vows?' It's like a trial run.

★ ★ ★

Poverty. The world says, 'Enough is not enough and you have to have as much as you can have, and if you want something, you should be able to go out and get it regardless of the effect that might have on other people.' Poverty says, 'With a simple amount, that can be enough, it can be more than enough.' That is what poverty means for me, not that we live in abject poverty. It is about living simply. And it is about giving up something. It is about giving up the chance to have a lot of material things that are nice to have. We do have 'things' and rooms, but we have nothing for the sake of having it.

With all the vows, particularly with poverty and with chastity, it all sounded all right on paper; and then my only Christmas that I've had so far in community I had letters from the friends that I was a student with. This friend is married; another friend is established in her job and has her own home. Another is in a great relationship. And it brought it home to me what I will be saying 'No' to. And I mind. You have to mind if it is important.

It is easy for your possessions to become part of your identity. The house you choose to live in, the way you choose to furnish it, the car, the clothes, they all say something about you. Being a sister here, I can still choose what I wear to a limited extent. We shop in second-hand shops. Personally, I don't enjoy shopping from second-hand shops and I try to buy the kind of things that I would have bought new. But inevitably I end up wearing things that are just OK, but I'm only wearing them because they've been given or were good quality. What am I saying?

When your identity does not include what you own, you have to be very true to yourself as a person. You have to know who you are more fully when you are not dependent on all those external things. I'm not trying to be a model of what 'a nun should be'. I am trying to be the person, as fully as I can be, that God is calling me to be. I'm trying to be me.

People have said that, 'If you took my home, my family, my car, my job, and everything I own, I would feel as if I didn't exist.' These things can get in the way of people discovering who they really are.

★ ★ ★

Celibacy. We do vow celibacy here. I'm not sure what chastity is: it sounds terribly medieval. But I know what celibacy is. It means no sex! I hope the consequence of this is not that I'm going to be some frustrated woman, but that it is a positive decision not to be involved in sexual relationships with men. When you are involved in a one-to-one relationship, it takes energy and commitment. With us that energy and love is given out to God, the Church and to the world. This does not mean that sex is wrong or bad. It is good. It is something that God made and delights in and has given.

If you are married in a true Christian context, you give your life to that one other person and you live your life out within the context of that one other person, making a family and a home in a particular framework. By vowing celibacy you can be used by God and by the community in a much wider context.

The fact that you vow celibacy does not mean that you become some sort of asexual being. I rejoice in the fact that I'm a woman (even if I get pre-menstrual tension and it's a pain). I feel very at home with my femininity and with my sexuality. Aside from being in a sexual relationship, everyone should be able to develop their own awareness of who they are and what it means to be a woman. For me being a woman means . . . Ah! I wish I hadn't said that because I'm not quite sure what it does mean, but I know I like it. It's something about enjoying my body and being aware that the body is beautiful just as it is. Things like being aware of the wind in my hair, the sun on my skin, the air on my face, a warm bath, enjoying the clothes that I choose to wear. The way all these things make me feel is part of me as a person.

I did have relationships before coming here. I had one that was very emotionally entangled and, although we didn't sleep together, it was really a sexual relationship. I found it difficult to get out, but I knew it wasn't right for me. It was an unhappy situation and I think it made me cagey about relationships. There were a couple of other relationships, but the idea of having a vocation was always very strong and I'm not the kind of person who could have superficial relationships. When I was training to be a nurse, there was a male nurse who really wanted to go out with me. I remember him sending a huge bouquet of flowers on Valentine's day and I was horrified. A friend said, 'He is absolutely infatuated with you', but I didn't feel the same way and I couldn't do relationships on that kind of level. And there was another man who expected me to sleep with him on the first date – he blew it!

If I did have sex with a man, it would be in the context of a loving relationship; I would be committed to that person and I would love them very deeply and it would probably be in the context of marriage. I didn't think, therefore, that it would be a good idea to give it a whirl just to see what I was missing!

★ ★ ★

Obedience. I see obedience as being about listening and being open to God and to your community and being prepared to be responsive to what you hear. I think being obedient is not like when you are a child – 'Make the bed now' and you go off and make it. It is a process of being prepared to listen and hear. The community as a whole undergoes that process and not just the individuals within it, so, if God is speaking to you, you can discern the right way forward with the community.

I can't see a situation where I feel God is calling me to do, say, a counselling course and the community say, 'The dishwasher is broken and we won't buy a new one because we've got a new novice.' The way it works is that we as a community listen to God and to each other and we listen to God speaking in each other. If it should ever happen that I felt God was calling me in one direction and the community was saying something different, I would simply tell Christine (we don't use the old language of 'Mother Superior') that I didn't feel that was what God wanted, and there would be a process of negotiation. If they were to persist that I was being called, for instance, to set up a house on Muroroa Atoll in the Pacific Ocean and I was to go and build it, I would say, 'Well I don't think this is what God is calling me to do.' I don't think they would say, 'Yes, it is.' But, if they did, I would go and try it out. But I don't think the community would ask me to do something that God wasn't asking me to do or that they didn't feel that God was asking me to do. Part of the novitiate is learning to trust the community, and I do trust the community here and I feel that together we can find the path that God is asking me to walk.

We haven't covered the vows yet in my novitiate classes, so what I've said might be totally different from what the community would say. It's just the way I see them at the moment from where I am. I just wanted to say that!

What I have here that I didn't have outside is the chance to have a deepening relationship with God. If I was outside and I had the chance to go to amazing places and see wonderful things, it would still all be part of my journey towards God, and my journey towards being a whole person and the person who God wants me to be. But this environment, for me, is the environment in which I can make that journey best. I actually see, since I've come here, the very rich experience. There is a depth and a meaning and a kind of rightness about it and it just is . . . very good.

It is very frustrating as well. At 6 a.m. when my alarm goes off, when I'm listening to another story that starts, 'You don't know what you are missing. When we were novices . . .' or on Fridays when I'm ploughing my way through cod's roe for dinner, then I think, 'Why am I here, God? Why am I doing this?' And yet I don't want to walk out.

I'm sure my parents would have liked to have seen me married and settled down with a family, but now they see me happy here they are going along with it. My brother, a doctor, is concerned about me 'shutting myself up in a convent' and is worried that I'll be old before my time, but I think, as he sees that I'm happy here, he'll accept it. A lot of friends who knew me before I came into the community and have known me since I've been here have said 'Rachel, you seem so happy. You seem so right.' They've been convinced by the reality.

Rachel has now completed her Diploma in Pastoral Studies. She has chosen to work for two days a week in a nursing home and for two days a week at Aston University where she works with the chaplains as a volunteer. Within the next year Rachel hopes to take vows for a further three to six years.

sister helen

*One chap at work turned round to me and he said,
'What? Do you mean to say they don't pay you and you
can't have sex?' and I said, 'Well basically, yes.'
He was utterly horror-struck.*

sisteſ нelen

*The convent where the OHP Sisters live has a breathtaking setting,
perched high up on a cliff with the sea clearly in view. The wind howls
around the convent with an almighty force. A bracing walk up the hill from
the local bus stop brings you into a traditional and beautiful convent with
shiny polished wood and stone pillars. If one were to select a community for
the aesthetics of the building alone this would be the one to choose.*

*The refectory has windows that look out over the hillside and the moors,
and as the sisters take lunch they listen to* The World at One *on
Radio 4. It is very incongruous and slightly humorous to hear the Prime
Minister's voice haranguing Parliament in the calm and peace-loving
atmosphere of the convent. And then, lunch over, he is suddenly
switched off in the middle of a sentence.*

*Sister Helen is thirty years old and has been a novice for two years. She is
wonderfully, joyfully down to earth; I wondered how the other sisters cope*

with such huge energy and vitality. She did not hesitate before speaking, or
worry about what the community might think, but seemed confident
that whatever she said they could handle.

I found her complete honesty about the problems of the novitiate very
courageous as I'm often seen as 'media-person-not-to-be-trusted'.
Helen chatted to me like a friend at the pub.

Jesus has absolutely captivated me, which is the reason I'm here. I didn't realise this when I came; it's only in the last year I've realised what's been going on. He has captivated me so much that I don't think there is room in my life for a 'significant other', which of course was tough on my boyfriend. I hate all this bridal imagery, I just can't cope with it. But when push comes to shove, I have to say that's what's going on. For me, prayer is being with Christ.

I was in my nine-to-five job, working as an archivist, which I love, and thinking that I felt quite called to prayer, a 'life of prayer' I suppose. Doing my job and being involved in the church wasn't enough; I needed something more. I thought, 'Well, I suppose that means I've got to become a nun!' and at that point I wasn't prepared to think about it because I was going out with someone and we were enjoying ourselves and I thought 'What am I going to tell Paul?' So I tried hard to forget about it.

I've never really understood what we mean by 'called' and I hate the word – although in a sense I suppose I was. The compulsion to come got so strong that I could no longer ignore it. It was almost like, whatever I did, it wasn't enough. But where does the inner compulsion come from? Is that the call? I don't know. I suppose it is. I suppose the Holy Spirit is moving something in you to get you moving out of this nice little rut that you've got yourself into, saying, 'Hey, you're never going to be happy doing this. Have you thought about this?'

I hate this thing about 'The Call'. Sometimes I think maybe there are certain people who are psychologically fitted to live in community and for whom this way of life is a way they can find fulfilment. Now, whether or not it is something deep in your psyche that responds to that and it comes up from your subconscious, or whether or not it is actually God picking you up by the scruff of the neck and saying 'Here, this is where I want you', I don't know. I suspect the two are so close that you can't divide them. Where does your unconscious begin and end? And how does that react with God working within you? I do believe that for anyone to explore a vocation to community can only be done through the power of the Holy Spirit.

I became a Christian through a Billy Graham rally, 'Mission England', when I was a student in Plymouth in 1984. I was nineteen, and I was confirmed in quite an evangelical church. Right from the beginning, whenever I've prayed, I somehow could never find the words, and I just used to end up sitting in what I thought was the presence of God. Trying to be in God's presence, trying just to find God and not to actively do anything at all. That was very natural to me.

My family were not religious and didn't go to church. I joined a local choir when I was eleven because I had a good singing voice, but I found it boring, and preferred lying in bed on a Sunday morning. Later on I was sent to a Quaker school, and although they have no creed, each day started with ten minutes' silence and once a week we had a meeting where we were all expected to sit still and quiet for forty minutes. There was no let up for the younger children, and of course we giggled, passed notes, whispered and nudged each other, but we were expected to sit still and maybe I learnt to appreciate the silence. In the evangelical environment of the church where I was confirmed, prayer was something you said out loud. I tried to be in the silence and to find God in that. I listened for God's voice, or what you think is God's voice.

I felt a terrific guilt complex because the evangelicals would tell me about all these wonderful prayers, and have these two-hour prayer sessions and all this intercession on behalf of everyone. And I'd think

'I don't do that.' I fall asleep after half an hour; I'd fall asleep after ten minutes and I just couldn't cope with all these words. And I'm thinking 'What's wrong?' because no one else seems to do this in my church, and it was only when I went to St Michael-le-Belfrey in York that I met someone else who felt the same way. I couldn't cope with those who seemed to spout at God, or whatever they did for two hours every morning, or did these wonderful meditations on Scripture or whatever.

I read that some people are led into charismatic gifts and some are led into silence and contemplation, and that was a revelation – as that is where I find God. Even now my natural way is just to sit and be. And that is what my prayer is, just being – being with – allowing him or her, just being with the Lord, however that may be – it may be resting or wrestling with, saying, 'I can't cope with this. What's going on? This is dreadful. What do you mean by this?' I find God in the silence, in the things around me and sometimes in the people around me.

My sense of the divine has been mainly through my experience. I'm the sort of person who naturally gets in touch with the world through my feelings. I'm an intuitive kind of person and I rely on my experience and how things feel, but now I'm using my intellect as well and making a discipline of study and reading.

And of course you'll say that sometimes God doesn't seem to answer prayer. And I think I've said prayers which haven't had an answer, and I struggle with this as much as anyone does. What I've come to in the last couple of years is that it's not for me to dictate the answer in my terms. And I don't know how God is going to answer, and when God is going to answer, and what you're going to do if the answer is not what you want and doesn't come in a form you want it or in a form you are expecting. And it may not come for twenty years. I don't know.

It's interesting – the relationship I have with my non-Christian parents is far closer now than it was. They have never stood in the way of my coming here, but they don't understand why I'm doing what I'm doing, really they don't. My dad is an accountant, my mum works in an office and my brother is a doctor, and we have never discussed religion. But I think it's a prayer of anyone whose parents are not believers, that they may have some sort of knowledge of God in their lives. I've been praying for this for years and years and years, and I'd almost given up. I'd carry on praying but not really expecting – and all of a sudden I see glimpses. Then it comes.

My prayer life here wasn't easy when I first came. The novitiate is pure hell. A lot of the stuff you go through right at the beginning, the letting go of what you've had: your old life, boyfriend, house, job, car, freedom and all your old expectations and assumptions. It is all gone. And what have you got to rely on? Well you've got yourself, and even your view of yourself is turned completely inside out and upside down, so you haven't even got that any more. So what do you rely on? Well, God's still there but God might be a concept, and your old ways of praying might not even work. Sometimes you have to rely on your head knowledge when times get tough, and I think perseverance, or stickability if you like, is the key to the Religious Life. It's easy to run away when life gets horrendous and everything seems to be black.

I've been asking what God wants me to do about whether to stay here for the next three years. I have to apply to the community who put it to the vote, and I have to have 75 per cent of the vote if I'm going to stay. I've been asking and asking God what to do, but I've been unable to discern all the different voices inside my head. In the end, I just gave it to God by stopping asking the question and just living and seeing what stays.

I'm not going to carry on asking God, but asking myself 'What do I really want? What does Helen really want with her life?' and bringing it before God in prayer. Do I want to be in this community or do I want to be out of it? And let's look at the realities of life outside . . . working from nine till five in the record office. Am I really going to be able to do what I want to do? Which is to have a life of prayer.

I just gave it time and let the thought and feelings bubble up, and I talked to a few people. I've got to the stage now where if they vote against me, I'll be upset but I actually won't mind. I got to the stage where I couldn't struggle with it any longer. So I'm back to just sitting with God in silence.

Then we have the luxury of being able to spend five services a day praying for the world. Every day I read the newspapers and just take it all into chapel with me. I don't have any answers, and I can't answer the famous question of 'Why does a God of love allow suffering?' Suffering can be totally disfiguring of someone's psyche and soul. I have had times of great pain but I've never had the great physical suffering that some people have to live with. I'd love to hear someone – perhaps someone who lives with chronic disability or is living in chronic pain – answer this, because I feel as if I'm incapable of giving an answer. I can only say 'This is how it seems to me.' It can be an ennobling thing but it can also be very very destructive.

I hope God doesn't send any suffering to anyone, even to bring good things out of it, but suffering is part of the human condition. I believe God created this world and also gave creation (sorry about the jargon) free will. God created good things, but the flip side of that is you get evil, things mutating, and you do get suffering. We can go through life expecting it all to be wonderful, but life just isn't like that. All I'd say is that I don't believe God sends suffering to you. Suffering might be on your life's journey, for whatever reason. You may well get cancer. It's a pure fluke that you've got cancer. Why you and not me? I don't know. I can't answer that question. But what I could say is that I believe God is with you in it.

The first eighteen months here, as I said, were pure hell, and even right at the bottom I'd say God was in it there somewhere. I was anorexic at one stage and could hardly eat anything and at the same time I was clinically depressed. That is the sort of suffering I know, but I think that, even through all that, God was there.

I think, looking back on my life, that I was probably chronically depressed earlier in life but I never had the chance to work it through. I am tall and I was horrendously bullied at school and, although home life with my parents and brother was happy, my parents do not show their emotions easily. I wonder now if there was almost a low level chronic depression which I didn't recognise and no one else recognised.

And it came out when I got here, because all the things that normally give you enough support to function outside were gone. I mean, I had a good job, a house of my own, a car, I had boyfriends, friends . . . they were all gone. And if what is inside isn't worked through, I think depression is inevitable. I think I was very detached from my feelings before, whereas now I've had to recognise all that and had to work with it and come to terms with it. I think my heart is engaged now.

My family are coming around to the idea of my being here now. My father turned round to me a while ago and said, 'Actually I'm quite proud of you for doing what you are doing.' As I said, my brother is a doctor and my cousin is a freelance journalist in London. My mother said that they are proud of me because I've had the guts to do something that none of them would have had the guts to do. I think that they understand now that this is not an easy choice. Of course, my mother would like grandchildren and she said, 'Oh Helen, can't you just be normal like everyone else and get married and have children?' I said, 'I want to give this a try. I don't want to get to forty and have regrets and be sitting in my job surrounded by computers and thinking, "If only I'd done it. If only I'd had a go." '

What really cracked it for me in the end and what made me come was thinking, 'Why don't you want to come?' And the reason was that I was scared of the idea. I was scared because it was very unfamiliar and I didn't think that was a good enough reason. 'You've got no dependants. If you're going to try, now is the time. If you wait until you are forty, it would be impossible to start again if it doesn't work. But if you give it a go now, you might just stand a chance.' I was twenty-eight when I first came and now I'm thirty. I'm glad I came when I did.

I'm very aware that I'm a woman, in a women's community which is basically in a male church which has been run by men for men. And I feel a great burden to redress the balance. My God isn't male. One of the big things for me in my first year in community is to realise that you are made in the image of God. And it's very easy to make the step, 'Well, if I'm made in the image of God . . .' I'm a woman, I'm very definitely a woman. So where does that leave God? God defies gender. For me it is quite natural and I find it quite liberating to use feminine images of God. She is glorious.

Poverty, Chastity and Obedience

Poverty isn't a big issue for me. We have 'things' in this community but we share them. It's about simplicity and stewardship. What I really miss is clothes. Even though we can wear mufti on days off, when we go out I really miss buying clothes. Before I came to community I weighed twelve and a half stone and I was quite large. Now I have a great figure and I'm thin and I can't even take advantage of it! I really miss colourful clothes, and that hurts inside. On days off I love wearing leggings or jeans and brightly coloured T-shirts.

When you go out in a habit, you have to be nice to everyone all the time, and being 'divine love' all day long is very wearing. The guy at the bus stop who has had too much to drink – everyone else just ignores him but you are the one person at the bus stop who has to acknowledge him and be loving. You can't say 'No'. But having said that, it can lead you into all sorts of interesting situations and interesting conversations with people. You are very available in a habit to the weirdos, the drunks and for anyone who just wants someone to talk to. It's a mixed blessing. But I love it when I can go out in outrageous colours – and I love buying clothes, I really miss that. And I miss going to the pub.

Not having a house doesn't bother me because the house was always a worry anyway. I've still got the house, but I'll be glad to get rid of it. To be honest, it's a millstone around my neck. And I miss having my own car and being able to get out. Well, sometimes I just itch to get out – but not as often as I thought I would. It's a real surprise because I was always a person for getting out and about and I was never a very 'geographically stable person'. I was never at home, whereas now I'm quite happy to be here.

★ ★ ★

Chastity is the real nub of the whole thing. People say 'How can you do it? How can you give up men?' Well, first of all, in this place one has to say that although we do have male visitors there are very few of what I would call 'objects of desire'. I don't think I have the hugest sex drive. It would be very interesting to talk to a sister with a very high sex drive and see how she coped. We vow celibacy here rather than chastity because we may have had sexual relationships in the past, as I have had. I think chastity was more about purity of heart or something – I'm not quite clear what it used to mean. I think married people can be chaste – I may well be wrong.

It is a problem. There are guys and you think 'Oh gosh, yes.' You can't switch your sexuality off and it's one of the big discoveries for me. Before I came to community, I was very un-switched on. I hadn't really fully come to terms with Helen as a woman, that this woman has breasts and was actually a sexual being who quite liked being around men and found men sexually attractive. I am more aware of it now and, when you know very well that you're in a place where you are never ever going to enjoy a man in that way again, it makes you think about it more. I've really had to come to terms with my sexuality as a woman to live a celibate life, because you can't switch it off. Coming to terms with it means being aware that I'm a sexual being, and that I can look at a guy and think 'I like you', and that is God-given. I think by switching your sexuality off you are denying something of God, because it is a gift God gives to us all. To switch off your sexuality is as much a denial of God's gift as misusing it in any way, or becoming promiscuous or using sex perhaps as a weapon or a way of crying out for help.

I've never been a promiscuous person; I've only ever had sex in the context of a relationship. It would be interesting to know whether anyone who has been very promiscuous and just enjoyed sex for its own sake in a very casual way could take a vow of celibacy. It is an interesting question, and I'd have to talk to people and try and find out. I did enjoy sex, but it was always in the context of a loving relationship. I don't think I could do it outside a relationship unless it really was 'lust at first sight'. I might actually think it, think lustful thoughts and enjoy it, but I don't know that I could go through with it. I've looked, though.

There is a line in one of the psalms that we sing in chapel, where David has written 'I take no delight in men's legs' – it's about human power or something, but it always makes me smile and I think 'Speak for yourself, mate!'

And I don't like the idea of not being able to have a child. That is hard for me. I'd love to have a child and be a mother. Friends of mine are now mothers and I think it must be a very special thing.

★ ★ ★

Obedience is hard. We all like to be in control. And coming to community you can't be in control. It's all about mutual responsibility and obedience. I don't have the foggiest idea what my work here will be. I might be professed in the autumn or they might throw me out. If I'm here, I don't know where I'll be after that. I haven't a clue. You do have some choice and they'll consult you. But I may be needed by the community to do something that I would not necessarily choose to do. For example, I am interested in feminist theology but it may not be appropriate for me to go off and do a study course, even if there is one which follows exactly my interest. But you can't automatically do that. For example, if I am at one of the smaller houses, then if I go off to study, I'm throwing more work on to them. You have to say, 'Is this OK?' If you want to do something really weird, they might say 'No'.

There is a sister at Wantage that went off to study aromatherapy and massage and now practises massage on the sisters. I would love to study something like that. I think it is a brilliant idea. A lot of the sisters here are into burning oils. When you walk around, you have all these wonderful scents of, say, ylang-ylang or petunia oil, which is lovely.

I'd have more to say about obedience if I was asked to do something that I really didn't want to do. But I don't anticipate that. They do ask and consult you, and in the end you say 'Yes' and go.

I find it difficult to verbalise what makes it worth it and why I'm doing what I'm doing. I sit in that chapel and I'm aware of God's presence around me, and I'm aware of this prayer. It's not always easy, and I read the newspapers and take it all in with me and it makes it all worth it. I suppose what I'm saying is that what I really want in my life is to be with God. It sounds very nebulous and very holy and that sort of thing but I really believe it's true. To have the time to be with God and to really live that in a way that you can't out there.

And to have the opportunity to go to chapel for our services, 'Offices' they are called . . . for morning, midday and evening prayer, compline and the Eucharist. The privilege of being able to pray four times a day with these people who sometimes I like and sometimes I don't, is wonderful. And that's why I'm doing it, for that privilege. Everything else comes from that. The hospital visiting, the parish work, everything all comes from the Office and the personal prayer.

It sounds horrendous, doesn't it? And totally pie-in-the-sky. I think of the Office as a job. Sometimes I don't want to be there and sometimes it is boring and sometimes it's tiring – but sometimes it's wonderful and the whole thing comes together. But I see it as a job that we have undertaken on behalf of the world, just to be in that chapel.

It is the psalms that are the richness, and I find through the psalms all sorts of images come into my mind: the violence, anger, joy, sadness. That in itself is a prayer. There are some psalms that always make me think of violence and some of the horrendous things that are happening: the terrorist acts, bombs going off in Barcelona airport or what has been going on in Bosnia, and the suffering that people live with there. And I think that the thoughts are a prayer. Maybe it's really for my own benefit and not for theirs but I don't believe that. I really believe that every prayer helps and that, somehow if we weren't there, in a sort of mystic way, the world wouldn't be such a good place to be in.

Shortly after this interview the community accepted Helen for a further three years.

At the time of going to press she is spending a year at the community's house in South Africa.

sister judith

*One day my family were all sitting discussing what we
had wanted to do when we grew up and someone said;
'When Judy was four she wanted to be a nun!' and
everybody roared with laughter, thinking this hysterically
funny. I thought 'Oh help, what am I going to do?'
I was twenty and I still wanted to be a nun.*

sister judith

When I first visited the Sisters of the Love of God I had not realised I was visiting an 'enclosed' community, but the difference was apparent as soon as I rang the bell. Sister Judith is thirty-three, and the only one of the sisters I met to have chosen to wear the old style 'wimple' which is the formal head-piece with a bandeau across the top of the head and an additional chin piece. This, along with the beautiful but floor-length brown habit, makes Judith look as if she has walked straight from medieval times. The community encourages a more informal style and Sister Judith will be the last novice allowed to wear this veil.

There is a wholeheartedness about the life here. They still rise in the middle of the night to say prayers between 2 a.m. and 3 a.m. Judith is not free to spend her holiday with her family and leaves the community only for medical reasons, or to attend religious conferences.

Judith had arranged for me to meet the Mother of the community who showed me around the grounds and gave me the impression that I was the only person on the planet, so complete was her attention to my every word.

I enjoyed interviewing Sister Judith very much despite the fact that she was at all times careful and guarded about what she said, feeling herself to be a representative of the Religious Life and of her community. I worried that she would decide at the last minute not to be included and am thrilled that her interview is here, and in full.

It can drive you absolutely bats, the seven services a day. The bell goes for chapel and you haven't had time to finish whatever it is you are working on. This should remind you that the primary thing is the prayer and not whatever project you have in hand. The day and night are punctuated by the services to remind you that the most important thing is the prayer and the glory of God. This is one of the reasons I chose this community, because it still has seven services. I need the continual reminders. Otherwise give me two hours and I'll have forgotten about God. I need to go back into chapel and remind myself what life is all about. Although I can swear when the bell goes because I'm not ready.

I come from an extended Hungarian family. My great-grandmother, grandfather and grandmother lived in the house when I was born. My uncle and aunt and three cousins were always around, so the house was always full. It was a very cosmopolitan upbringing and we always had visitors from Hungary and from all over the world, particularly Brazil, Sweden, Switzerland – contacts and people came from everywhere. They didn't all speak English but we all communicated without any problems. I was brought up with many different cultures around me; we were always being fed and it was very friendly and relaxed. Hospitality was always there; guests found it as they found it and if there were too many people, children started sleeping on the floor. The flavour of life was very happy.

My parents weren't churchgoers. My mother used to go to the

8 a.m. service three times a year at Christmas, Easter and Whitsun. If you were up early enough and dressed, without her having to get you up and dressed, then you were allowed to go with her, so I used to make supreme efforts to be up and ready. And the best bit of being a Brownie Guide was that you had to go to church once a month. Once I was a Brownie I had an excuse and I used to go with a neighbour. It was the local Church of England church but I was desperate to go. It's strange, isn't it? One of my prized possessions, which I cringe when I look at now, was a terribly Victorian picture of Jesus, a long white dress type, which the local church sent on the anniversary of my baptism. They sent a card like this every year and I kept them lovingly in a box of all my 'treasures'.

The Hungary my father grew up in was very antisemitic. In 1944 the Nazis invaded Hungary and by that stage they had learnt exactly how to round people up and send them away, and statistically they made a better job of it in Hungary than they did anywhere else. By the time I was born, my father's views on religion were 'I don't mind what you think as long as you don't force your ideas on anyone or kill anybody for not being what you are.'

I went to the local 'Mixed Infants' and then to an independent grammar school. I was a musician and played the violin in local orchestras. I remember admitting twice that I wanted to be a nun. I once told a chemistry teacher, who asked me what I would do if I didn't teach the violin. I said, 'I want to be a nun.' I remember her reaction, amazed bewilderment, and 'Well, that's quite another kettle of fish!' At fourteen, I was praying devoutly that God would ask me to be anything except a nun. By sixteen it hadn't gone away. I went to the Royal Academy of Music for three years and then did a teacher training qualification in music and chemistry. In my second year at music college I came here to visit. They told me I was too young (I was twenty) and that I must have a minimum of two years' work experience. So I had two more years of music college, and then I got a job teaching violin and chemistry and then I came back.

They said: 'Well if you really want to go ahead, spend a month at one of our smaller houses.' I did that and decided there was no way I was having anything to do with the Religious Life. I went away and had a brilliant three years, a new job and a new lease of life. Then I realised that I had missed out by not learning how to pray. So I planned to come here for a year and go away again. I managed to persuade the local county to give me a sabbatical year to come here for nine months, and go and work with Mother Teresa for three months. The problem was that after three months I realised that this was what I wanted to do with my life.

Last night I dreamt the alternative ending. I dreamt I went back after my sabbatical year and met the children that I'd been teaching. But that isn't what happened. I went to India and worked in a children's home. And what that showed me is that I wanted to come back here. Of course 'doing good works', feeding the poor and looking after the sick is wonderful work, but for me it doesn't get to the root of the problem. The problem is people's selfishness and greed, and if you are going to start tackling that you need to be in a place like this – rather than mopping up the effects of selfishness. Not that I mean to denigrate in any way the mopping up process; there need to be people doing that, but I feel my calling is to be here, despite the fact that I love to be out there helping people. You start by dealing with the selfishness and greed in yourself.

I heard a tape of Thomas Merton's last address before he died. It is wonderfully inspiring and describes how he sees the monk's relationship to the world by talking about a statue of the Buddha. The Buddha sits with the begging bowl in one hand and touching the earth with the other hand. This refers to when the Buddha became enlightened, and when that happened he was sitting on a little square of earth. Mara, the equivalent of the devil, came and said: 'I own this piece of ground on which you are sitting', and the Buddha touches the ground (Buddhists may not agree with this) because he is calling the earth to witness that he has gained enlightenment on this square of earth and that the devil doesn't have any right to it. The earth is liberating him but also he is liberating the earth by gaining his enlightenment on it. That is the work of the contemplative monk or nun – to struggle to achieve that liberation for the world. We are here on behalf of the world and for the world and if we manage to gain enlightenment or holiness, it is for the world's liberation that we do that.

As to whether I was 'called' . . . I can tell you what I *don't* believe. I do not believe God sits in heaven and says: 'Right, well, there is Theresa and there is Mary and, ah, Judith – she's going to be a nun.' And I sit down here and I either become a nun, in which case God ticks the box, or I don't, in which case God crosses the box; and when I come before him on judgment day he'll say: 'Go to hell because you weren't a nun.' That is not how I see it.

So, called? You are called by circumstances, what's inside you, your experience and what best liberates you to be most completely you. In my case there has always been an intuitive something that has said: 'You are to be a nun.' That may just be an intuitive wisdom that knows that this is how I can best respond, but equally, like in the dream I was telling you about, the alternative ending to my sabbatical year could equally have been a possibility and would have been equally right and been equally my calling.

I shy away from this 'called' because it gives the idea that there is one particular way and that's it. I think God is much more fluid than that. There isn't one way to be a tree; every tree and every leaf on every tree, even every leaf on the same tree is different – that is the diversity of God. And all cherry trees aren't exactly the same. They are all called by God to be cherry trees but they do it differently and we are dealing with that kind of a God, so the question isn't: 'Has Judith become a nun or not?'

It is infuriating that people see this life as sacrificing our freedom. If I was sacrificing my freedom, I wouldn't be doing this. I come from a family that have lived under communist rule; some of them didn't come out until 1956, and I have been brought up to value my freedom very highly. There are moments when you think of what you've 'given up' and it is only honest to admit that, but I am not in any way sacrificing my freedom. If people see it like that, they are seeing and believing in an illusion. Freedom is not the freedom to go off on holiday, to travel, to do what I want when I want. That actually isn't freedom. If anyone looks at us from outside and thinks: 'Well she can't say "I want to go to Switzerland tomorrow", therefore she has sacrificed her freedom.' Well, freedom doesn't consist of that.

At our profession, when we make our vows, the person who receives them says to us: 'Sister Judith, what do you desire?' and the response is: 'I desire the mercy of God and liberty to bind myself to him in a life of prayer and reconciliation in this community.' It is the 'liberty' that is important, I want the liberty to be able to commit myself completely to God. Liberty and freedom is the ability to see the illusions and not to go along with them. The liberty not to think 'They are cutting off my freedom because I can't go on holiday.' Part of freedom is accepting and using the limitations that your choice imposes. I chose circumstances which to the world outside may appear to sacrifice my freedom, but I hope they will make that inner liberty a reality in me.

And one more thing about choice. All choices are limiting in some way. If you go to a party, you are not free to go to the cinema. What matters is accepting and using the attendant limitations on your choices.

True freedom is an inward thing. A compelling example is Maximilian Kolbe; he was totally un-free, in a concentration camp, yet the degree of inner liberty he showed, by choosing to die in place of another prisoner, is a freedom no captor could take away from him.

The idea some people have of the enclosed life is that there is a line drawn around the convent we can't step over. We have to share responsibility for that. A lot of old convents would have had barbed wire and whatever to stop people from getting in, and they didn't step over the line and go out in the way that we go out, but that is not what 'enclosure' is about. Just as being able to do what I want when I want does not constitute freedom. Enclosure is declaring a sacred space. This space is where I'm going to pray and seek God with all my life. In this particular community I can't go home and see my family. Most communities can; it is just the way that this particular community understands enclosure.

God is what we are seeking and 'the kingdom of God', to put it into gospel words. The divine intention is what we really want to be in tune with, what we want to be flowing with, and anything else is actually getting in the way. Can I try and explain that again?

Perhaps peace is a better word. God desires the peace and harmony of the whole of creation, that is 'the kingdom', that is what God desires. The incarnation, God becoming man, and the cross are the necessary means to enable the creation to come to peace and harmony. That capacity has been given us, but we also have free will not to use it. We often choose not to use it, or we collude with not seeing it, particularly when it means cost to ourselves.

We can be aware of that peace and the possibility of it flowing, and somebody can come along and hurt you. You have a choice; you can either think, 'But what I want is the peace and the harmony to flow and so I'm not going to get involved in hurting back.' Or you can hurt back. Nine times out of ten we hurt back – therefore we are colluding with not seeing what real peace is about because we don't want the cost of it.

In the convent we seek peace of heart. We say 'This is what we want to do', but we don't do it half the time, like everybody else. But we are committed, and the fact that we are living this life brings us up constantly against the places where we don't do it. It is very painful when you are not in tune with that peace, and aware that you are not in tune with it. When that happens there is always something of self that you are wanting to protect.

If someone hurts you, it is easy to think 'Well, they are actually in the wrong here, so I have every right to say so', so you speak out against it. The cost of saying 'But I really want peace' is too great, so you attack in some way, justifying, 'Anyway they were wrong.' It goes on here just like it goes on everywhere else.

My views on God are changing all the time. They should always be changing because you can't ever know him. And I object to 'him' – 'her' is no better. Whatever we say isn't right, so I stick with the convention and say 'him'. I would hope that my knowledge of God has deepened, but I don't think it is a very safe thing to try and measure. God is faithful, and if you are faithfully seeking, God will be faithful to that seeking.

Once I moaned to a friend that you come here seeking God and what you really want is to feel God, and to know that you are feeling God, and to know that you are making progress towards God; you want that security. And shouldn't he jolly well give it to you, because after all you have come here? But what do you get? A total absence of God, you can't find God anywhere.

The friend replied to this that absence is an experience of God, but it isn't the one you wanted! You can come here and find that on the feeling level you can experience God much less than you do outside, but just because you don't 'feel' God doesn't mean that you don't experience him.

The experiences that make me aware of God are very very varied; they are different every day and they don't come every day. At the moment, it seems to be by actually 'seeing'. And by that I mean walking past a rose bush that is planted outside the fruit store every day – and one day you actually 'see' the rose. You are struck by it and by its beauty and its smell and the sheer loveliness, and you are aware that God created it, and put it there. This particular rose bush that I'm thinking of has hundreds of little buds, and they all open out and they all look much the same when you are not really 'seeing' them, and then suddenly you see one. It will be there today and gone tomorrow and God bothers about it. The rose vibrates, and you vibrate with it. We can feel the beauty of the rose, like deaf people hear music. Evelyn Glennie, the deaf musician, says she experiences sound not through her ears but through her whole body. I think I experience joy from the rose in the same way – the whole thing vibrates and so do I. That is one way I experience God, seeing roses or seeing the sunlight in the trees. It is something we miss most of the time – we don't actually 'see'.

I'm also struck by the continual mercy of God, of being forgiven, of not being given up on, when you don't go along with the peace that I was describing earlier. The mercy of God is endless. And if a reader doesn't believe in God, God still goes on caring for them and creating them. I don't believe that God creates, like setting a top spinning and then leaving it to get on with it. God continues to create us. I am only here tomorrow if God continues to create me. For the person who doesn't believe in God, it is the same. God doesn't say, 'Well, that's it, Joe Bloggs doesn't believe in me, so I'm not going to go on with him. He'll cop it tomorrow.' God continues to create Joe Bloggs and continues to peep out at him through the roses and whatever else he might or might not see. And God longs – with infinite longing and far more love than I can ever imagine – for Joe Bloggs. And one day I believe Joe will die and see God, and realise how much God has loved him.

I experience God in the bread and the wine of the communion service. I don't think anybody can define this area, but it is not like the bread and the wine at Tesco. Something has happened. I experience God through the bread and wine, even if that experience is that it seems as if God is not in the bread and wine. As I said earlier, that too is an experience of God.

A priest once described it to me like this: he had a ring which he had been given at the service where he had been made a priest, and he had worn it all through his ministry. It was scratched and battered but it was his ordination ring. He said that with computer technology you could make an exact replica down to the scratches, but the copy would not have been present when he had been made a priest. He explained that even if he were to lose the ring he would not want a replica because it would not be the same. As if the first ring had somehow taken something in and was changed, the material thing was changed, by being present when he was made a priest in the way the replica wouldn't be. The same kind of change happens with the bread and the wine. I can't explain it better than that.

Then there is prayer. We are given two hours of prayer time a day here. The number one rule about prayer is to get down and do it – it's a bit like violin practice, you don't get better by thinking about it. It is easy if you have a wonderful time in prayer to think: 'That was great', and try to do it again. But every prayer time is new. It is easy in prayer to look for a good experience, instead of looking for God.

In this community I am able to be helped by sisters to pray in many different ways. I have learnt to pray with icons or with rosary beads or with my whole body and movement. I have learnt to use rhythmic prayer where one phrase is repeated many times. The words themselves are what you want to express but the repetition takes you to a different place, like the use of a mantra. I have been given good practical advice on prayer like 'Make sure that your body posture is not going to send you to sleep.' You have to be comfortable and with a straight spine so that you can maintain a position without having to shift and wriggle all the time. Then you just remember that God urgently, longingly and lovingly desires to communicate him/herself to you. You just sensitize yourself to God, or rather let God sensitize you, which is probably best done in silence, and then just notice the change. Notice that when you get up you notice the rose bush that you didn't notice before. It is a practical thing and you have to do it. The only way to pray is to pray.

Poverty, Chastity and Obedience

Poverty. Well, yes, I had a flat, I still have it because we are not allowed to dispossess ourselves of our property until we are in life vows, so I still have somewhere to go if I decide not to renew my vows.

But, of course, poverty isn't about having no money. Poverty according to our Rule is 'an entire dependence on Christ'. This has an expression in material things. I don't get a salary and I have no money to spend, but the purpose of the vow of poverty is to increase our dependence on Christ. To think that we have security in money or possessions is an illusion. The vow liberates you from those compulsive dependencies and enables you to find your entire dependence on God. Part of the vow of poverty is about realising the way you don't go along with the path of peace, the poverty of your nature, if you like. Doing that isn't a negative thing – 'Oh how awful I am' – but a joyful opportunity to experience the endless mercy of God. That's one way in which we realise our dependence on God little by little.

I have beautiful clothes, I'm very well dressed. And when things wear out they are miraculously replaced by the sister in the workroom. It might be different if the community was so poor that it couldn't afford to give me a new habit when my habit wore out, or I was cold because they couldn't afford a jumper. Poverty does not mean, and does not glamorise, the kind of poverty of people who do not have any clothes and are cold. The vow of poverty does not mean poverty of this kind is good in any way at all.

Where the vow pinches me most is in not having anything material to give. Not being able to buy my sister anything for her birthday. It's hard not being able to give presents especially on birthdays and at Christmas.

★ ★ ★

Chastity. Well, before community, I did have friends who were boys, but I didn't have boyfriends. Only a small part of chastity is about not having sexual relationships. It means more than the fact that I won't be going to bed with anybody. Again our Rule says that chastity is our 'whole being set upon God'. It means that I desire God with the whole of my being and that does include the sexual part. A vow of chastity certainly includes working out your own sexuality, it is just in a rather different setting from society's.

If you love somebody enough to have a sexual relationship with them, then you are attentive to that person, that one other. A celibate diffuses that attentiveness to everyone they meet. We have the capacity as humans to be attentive, and in people who have taken a vow of chastity that attentiveness is given to every person that they come into contact with. Or that is what we are aiming at. That capacity, which in most people will take expression in a sexual relationship, is being used, but in a different way.

Obviously the pressure from society to believe that sex is everything puts a great deal of pressure on us. That pressure makes me question: 'Am I completely up the spout?' or, more disturbingly, 'Am I cutting myself off from something that is actually essential?' But I'm not cutting that bit off, just using it differently. When you give that attentiveness to someone, that can also be wonderful.

You do not bury your sexuality in community and you don't pretend it's not there. And you certainly don't say it's wrong. Many of us in society have been brought up, either consciously or unconsciously, to believe that this area of our being is somehow dodgy, unholy or unclean. Both inside and outside community we have to let go of that and actively work against those ideas by rejoicing in the God-givenness of our sexuality. It is necessary to say 'no' to any areas of fear about sexuality, and definitely 'no' to anything that tells you that it is un-holy or 'not quite God', that God and sexuality don't mix. This is crazy, because it is God-given.

Some people, to my amazement, still think that we don't have male visitors here all the time. It would be very disturbing if we didn't have male visitors, because that would be saying that we needed to be protected in some way. This would be going along the lines again that there is something ungodly that we would need protecting from!

Of course my body longs to have children, that is part of its creation. I'm a thirty-three-year-old woman . . . It's very difficult. I said to a sister once 'I'm dying to have children, so obviously I'm not meant to be a nun, am I?' expecting the answer 'No dear, so go away and forget about being a nun', which is what I wanted. There was a long pause and she then said 'I don't think you could be a nun if you didn't have that part of you. The part of you that longs for love and longs to have children is the part of you that will make a good nun as well.' I think that is a true answer.

Not all women want to have children, but all nuns don't necessarily fit neatly into that box – at least this one doesn't!

★ ★ ★

Obedience comes from a Latin word meaning to listen. To listen you have to be obedient to circumstances as well as people. And God comes to you in circumstances and people, so in doing that you are listening to God too. Every time somebody asks you to do something and you want to do it a different way you notice how bloody-minded you are. Or maybe I should say I notice how bloody-minded I am. Having to do tiny little things other people's way drives me nuts! Obedience makes you notice how strong-willed you are and how you may not be using that strong will to be one with peace in other areas. Obedience shows you where your will is.

You have to ask yourself 'What have I come here to do?' and what you've come here to do is seek God, not get your own way. When there is discord and someone wants you to do something their way, you learn to ask yourself 'What am I really seeking?' and when you see what you are really seeking, then resisting doing it their way is an irrelevance, you just get on with it.

When I made my first vows, a friend who had known me before coming into community read this poem, written by a young soldier in the Second World War, who is being taught how to use a rifle. He said he'd chosen it because of the contrast so wonderfully drawn between work and the uselessness of beauty. It is 'Naming of Parts' by Henry Reed. May I read it to you? . . .

Today we have naming of parts. Yesterday,
We had daily cleaning. And tomorrow morning,
We shall have what to do after firing. But today,
Today we have naming of parts. Japonica
Glistens like coral in all of the neighbouring gardens,
   And today we have naming of parts.

This is the lower sling swivel. And this
Is the upper sling swivel, whose use you will see,
When you're given your slings. And this is the piling swivel,
Which in your case you have not got. The branches
Hold in the gardens their silent, eloquent gestures,
   Which in our case we have not got.

The contemplative life is about that uselessness of beauty. In some way it is unjustifiable. From the point of view of 'Am I feeding the hungry?' – No, I'm not, but I hope our life is beautiful and that some people will see it and the God it is pointing to.

When I visited the nursing community of St Mary at the Cross in Edgware in London, it was great. I absolutely loved the nursing and wondered:'Why shouldn't I do this?' What brought me back here was partly the realisation that I justified myself by the work. I often met people when I worked in the hospice who thought they were useless if they couldn't do anything any more.

And you could look at the cross like this. Christ chose to die because it was more creative than all those good works that we could have told him he'd be better off doing. To go on preaching and healing the sick looks far more useful to the world. But actually, dying was the most creative option. In dying he showed through his action that the love of God doesn't even stop at being nailed to a cross. God's desire for the peace and harmony of all creation is not broken by torture and death.

I picked up a book the other day by somebody who was tortured by the Japanese and has gone back recently and met one of the people who tortured him. He said, 'Hatred has to stop.' It was an incredibly moving book that is also saying that the desire for peace and harmony is stronger and greater and better than death and torture. And that other people apart from Jesus are part of that.

And why is there suffering in the world? Well, 'I don't know' is the honest answer, but I can tell you how I try to make sense of it myself. We tend to think that God hasn't got it right if there is suffering in the world, but we are called to believe and trust in him. In a sermon recently I heard the passage in Job, 'when God created the world the morning stars sang and the angels shouted for joy'. The preacher went on to point out that the angels might well not have shouted for joy – they might well have questioned the whole proceedings, asking whether it was right to do this. They could have asked, 'If you let something exist and give it freedom to be itself, aren't you making trouble for the future? And it will increase our workload! It will involve doing things entirely outside our job description until now. We are not rejoicing, we are complaining. If you had asked us we should never have agreed with your going ahead with creation and giving beings distinct from yourself freedom like this.'

We can laugh, but that is the attitude we are taking, we are saying to the creator, 'You haven't done this right – there is suffering in the world, so you can't have made it right.' Whatever the amount of suffering there is, God is in that suffering and suffers with us. I'm not saying that God approves of suffering. What appeals to us is that God should step in and stop all suffering happening. But that isn't the way God is dealing with it and we have to trust him that his way is actually the best way of dealing with it. I'm not saying I do this. I often tell God that the world is all wrong, but what that sermon is saying is that we have to believe in God. A great deal of faith is required. But don't let anyone interpret that as saying that I think suffering should exist or that suffering is good, or that God doesn't suffer in our suffering. I think God weeps. But God's way with the suffering is not our way. We want God to step in immediately because we can't bear it. And somehow God's way is different. Also part of God's way of dealing with it was to suffer himself as Christ.

I love the life here. I love the wholeness of the contemplative life and the God-directedness of the whole life. That is very freeing and what I've come for. We have a working garden and we grow our own fruit and vegetables. I love the tie with the land, touching the soil and harvesting the fruits of the earth. It's a gentle sensitising to the seasons. Before, I knew where we were in the calendar by school holidays. Now it's more by gooseberries and raspberries.

I have my violin and sometimes I'll play a baroque sonata with an accompanist. In my holidays, two weeks a year, friends come with a car stacked full of music and we sing. Despite the seriousness of this interview I do have fun in community. Everyone always comments about the joy and the twinkle in my eyes. A sister told me there is an Arab proverb that when there is a twinkle in the horse's eye it is a blessing on the household. She changed it to say that a twinkle in Sister Judith's eye is a blessing on the community. But don't write that will you?

At the time of this interview Judith had been in community for four and a half years. She hopes to have taken her life vows within three years.

sister lynn

One friend at work said, 'She's just running away from the world', and another really laid into him and said, 'Listen. This isn't running away! It's the hardest thing that she's ever done.' And it is interesting because the second friend isn't religious in any way but she knew this isn't an option that counts as 'running away'.

sister Lynn

COMMUNITY OF THE SISTERS OF THE CHURCH

RICHMOND, ENGLAND

Sister Lynn is thirty-three and has been a novice for two years. She is physically slight, and by nature a quiet and, I thought, rather a private person. I can't imagine what she would have thought when first asked by her community whether she would like to give an interview. She began by being rather serious, which always frightens me, but by the end of the interview I wanted to stay longer. I felt Lynn was really only comfortable when we stopped talking about her and talked about the spiritual life.

The huge convent, on Ham Common, has a modern chapel, a conference room which can comfortably house thirty people, and fourteen guest rooms for individuals or groups who come for rest and silence or just to enjoy a day in the beautiful, four-acre gardens in which Lynn and I sat to talk.

The rising bell goes at 6 a.m. If you are the one that is ringing it, you have to get up before that and not be late. We start with a Communion service in the chapel at 6.40 a.m., followed by half an hour's meditation and then breakfast. Then we have the next service, the morning Office, at 8.20 a.m. and then we all meet together to find out what the plan for the day is. We are sixteen of us here at the moment, from a community of, I think, about ninety sisters in various parts of the world. This meeting finishes about nine. Then we start work, which for me, here in the novitiate, is mainly housework of some kind. Morning tea is at 10.30 a.m. and then the novices have classes together from 11.15 a.m. until 12.15 p.m. The classes cover all aspects of our life – from prayer to the history of the community. On Fridays we have an outside lecturer who comes in, and anyone can come to these lectures. The last series we had was with a rabbi who came to speak about the psalms.

The midday service is followed by dinner and washing up. The afternoons for the novices, technically speaking, are given over to private study. We have a reading list which we are supposed to get through in two years, which I am barely a quarter of the way through. One or two afternoons are spent in 'ministry' work of some kind. One afternoon I work as a volunteer at a local stable where they do riding for the disabled, which is rather nice, another afternoon I help at a local 'drop-in' centre doing drama workshops with the mentally ill. I have done drama in the past, so I enjoy this. We did a pantomime at Christmas and they all really loved it. That was quite challenging but good fun. These are people who have had various kinds of mental illness and may have been hospitalised and I am really there as an enabler to help them overcome their nervousness about acting in front of each other. Sometimes I am the only leader there and then I am the one coming up with the ideas to keep them going. I don't really have a lot of experience. I used to belong to an amateur dramatic group and we put plays on but this is different, and I enjoy it.

Afternoon tea is at 4 p.m. It is optional, but is a chance to talk to guests. Our evening service is at 5 p.m. followed by an hour's prayer, meditation and/or spiritual reading. Then supper at 7 p.m. After supper there is sometimes time for us to meet together as a community and relax. Then we finish with our last service at 8.40 p.m.

I have two brothers, one older and one younger, and we were brought up in a house just outside Reading which was built on a new housing estate the year before I was born. At the time there were fields and farm land. It has now all been built on, but when we were kids we had plenty of places to play. My father worked as an architectural technician, first of all in London and then in Wokingham, much closer to us. My mother was a housewife and concerned to be there for the kids. She got a part-time job in a boys' home once we were all established in school, and was always there when we got home.

I was the spoiled one. I enjoyed that and I'm grateful that my brothers have forgiven me. I went to the local council primary school and then to the local comprehensive until I was eighteen. I wouldn't say that I loved school but I don't think I hated it; it was just one of those things that you had to do. I was given the choice to go to a grammar school the same as my older brother had done, but I chose the comprehensive because that is where my friends were going and I certainly wouldn't have wanted to go to a private school.

My parents were not churchgoers. Mum would come to a nativity play but Dad would only set foot in the church for a wedding or a funeral. One of my neighbours had a son of the same age and took us to church from about the age of three. Every so often we rebelled and said, 'Why do we have to go to Sunday school? What's the point?' I don't remember learning anything at all, but I went until I was about thirteen. Then I asserted my rights saying, 'Stephen left Sunday school when he was twelve so why can't I?' Then I found I missed it and went back, mostly for the companionship of the other kids. It certainly wasn't the teaching, because I never took any of it in. It was a highish C of E church but we never actually went to the services unless it was Harvest Festival or something.

Then, when I was about fourteen, suddenly God became real. I can't say how exactly. I was going through a really unhappy time at school. Who I was didn't match their standards – with who I was. I was different. I didn't necessarily choose not to conform or anything. It was hard. Sometimes, when you are fourteen, something as simple as falling out with your friends seems really important and major. At the time that was really hard to take, especially for me as I was shy and not easily able to make new friends. I needed something to hold on to and there was God.

Being forced, in a sense, to hold on to God made me realise that God was real and I must do something about it. When the vicar approached me and asked me if I'd like to be confirmed, I had already made up my mind and said 'Yes' straight away. Then I went home and told my parents with a 'this-is-what-I-want-to-do-and-you're-not-going-to-stop-me' attitude. A sort of reverse rebellion. I always do things backwards. I think they were surprised because they had no notion that I was 'religious', but they didn't stand in my way. Being an active member of the church was my rebellion against the people at school and what I had grown up with.

I got through my Os and three As but I didn't get the grades that I would have needed to go to a good university and my dad was against polytechnics. So, after seven months on the dole, I got a job in the Berkshire library service. I was moved around and promoted into three or four different jobs within the service and I ended up staying with them for eleven years. I earned a good salary and I used to go abroad on holiday almost every year. I went to Africa, Mexico, Jerusalem, and often to Europe. I love Switzerland and Italy. And I went to Thailand to visit my brother, who was living there.

It wasn't until I visited a monastery in my early twenties and loved it that the vague idea of being a nun crossed my mind. But I didn't want it. So I didn't think about it. As far as I was concerned, I was going to be normal and get married and have kids. The only nuns I ever saw when I was young were old – or they seemed to be. I had no notion that young people did that kind of thing.

I went to see my vicar and asked, 'What happens if God wants me to do this and I don't want to do it?' And so he said, 'Go away and pray about it.' And so I went away – and I didn't.

I thought maybe that, if I didn't think about it at all, it would go away. And so for years I didn't think about it. And it would go away and I'd be getting on with my life and then suddenly it would get in the way. Eventually I thought 'Well, if I don't do something about it, I'm never going to know, one way or another. If I start looking at it, maybe that will make it go away.'

At the time I'd have thought, yes, it was a 'call'. This was when it became a definite prospect instead of a vague idea. It became something to run away from. I was twenty-four when it first became a serious possibility, and twenty-eight when I finally acted on it.

It is hard to define 'call', because in order to do that you have to define God or the one who is calling and that is virtually impossible as far as I can tell. At the time, given my understanding of God, I would have said I believe that God was calling me. I would have felt extremely presumptuous to say, 'I've been called to be a nun.' I would have found that an extremely presumptuous thing to say. And I don't know; it was something that at the time I wouldn't have said came from inside me, but now I think . . .

The trouble is that my ideas of who I am and who God is have radically changed over the last couple of years. So it is hard to say now what I thought then. Now I think – this might sound a bit heretical, I don't know – I think that 'God', whoever God is for anybody, is the deepest longing of a person's being. So that if God was saying to me 'do this', supposing God isn't somebody 'out there', totally separate from me, but was the deepest longing of my being, then it must have come from me. And not from someone out there who was separate.

This is not something that I've ever tried to formulate into words because it is something that is growing. Now I don't see the two as separate, but that might change again in the course of my life. Now I believe God to be my deepest longing and the fulfilment of that longing. So God, whoever God is, would be encouraging me to choose the way of life that would most fulfil that longing. And that, therefore, in a sense, is a call. But it is not necessarily a call to the Religious Life but a call to be most fully who I am – and whatever the best way of my doing that is, to find out that way. I don't know if that makes any sense.

For me as a teenager, God was somebody who was like a champion, someone who is always ready to lift me out of whatever mess I had got myself into, or to stand up for me or comfort me if I needed comforting. Like a parent/child relationship I suppose. And I found it quite painful to realise (it was something to do with the resurrection story and the ascension story) that Jesus had stopped being a human being who was physical, like, say, my brother, who I could relate to on an outside basis. It was a while before I could realise what was meant by 'the Holy Spirit being a part of me'. I could have quoted you verses out of the Bible that said that I had been 'filled with the Holy Spirit' and that I was a 'temple of the Holy Spirit', but without knowing what it meant. To actually claim that a part of God is inside me and a part of me is a part of God is something that I felt difficulty with because I wanted God outside me to pick me up when I fell down. I suppose in a sense I saw God as some kind of a dictator, telling me that God has a path in life that he wants me to follow. Therefore, if I don't follow it, I'm in problems because I've only got myself to blame if it goes wrong. However, I now think, more, that God isn't quite so drastic as that anyway, but that God is much more a part of me. The fact of saying, 'I've been filled with the Holy Spirit' means that therefore I have no excuse to say 'No, I can't do anything.' Because within me is God, so I must have the resources to deal with whatever life throws at me. Before I would have said, 'No, I can't do that' and denied responsibility. Somehow it is a tremendously wonderful thing, to have God as part of me, or me as part of God . . . But that makes me responsible for what I do, and I can't blame somebody else. But as I say, this is all very much in process at the moment, so it probably doesn't make any sense at all. God is within me as well as around me and is calling me – again there is that word calling, leading me on to become the fullest that I can become. This interview is hard work!

My experience of God has grown through experiencing love from other people since I've been in community. Not that I didn't experience love from other people before, but I didn't equate it, ever, with anything to do with God. Whereas living in an environment like this you tend to equate things more with God because God is talked about more. Certainly I would say that I have learnt more about God through relationships and people than I have through lectures and classes. They have their place, but the deeper learning is done outside of the classroom.

The simple fact of leaving a job that I'd known and an area that I'd known and people that I had known virtually all my life and moving to a different area was scary enough to make me appreciate the love that I was shown – not just by the sisters but by other people that I worked with outside the convent. To an extent I was able to accept myself more. I suppose I would say that was what God desired for me, that I grow in acceptance of myself, and of other people, and to grow in love. Experiencing the love of other people, both giving and receiving, is the way that we experience the love of God, I think. Because that is how God acts – through people. How you experience the world is how you experience God.

I pray in lots of different ways. Once or twice I have been given experiences which have given me something to work towards, to live towards. The only words I can give you to describe it is 'a total experience of the love of God'. I know it's a cliché, but I just don't have words that could be adequate.

On a more daily level, there are the 'help' prayers when I'm doing something wrong, which is usually in the kitchen. There is the daily Office in chapel. There is the silence which is difficult to sustain but profoundly powerful sometimes, and then anything I do that is creative is a kind of prayer. I do photography and calligraphy and I think that is partly an offering and partly allowing the creator to work through you. Then there is intercession and other kinds of prayer that you don't even realise is prayer. God definitely has a sense of humour and you have to be careful what you ask for. People pray for patience and then they are given all sorts of ways to develop it. It is very hard for me to say to anyone 'Of course God answers prayer' without knowing that person's experience, and how that person is praying or what their concept of God is. All I can say is that my experience has been that God does answer prayer. You may not like the answer you get or it may not be obvious or it may not come at once, which may sound like a bit of a cop-out, but it's the best way I can say it.

Then there is the presence of suffering, about which I have read any number of books. I think for starters I really believe that any amount of suffering that we go through causes God far more pain than we can imagine. And far more pain than we can experience, because God is that much bigger than us. Of course, the standard question is 'Why doesn't God step in and stop it?' There is something in there about allowing us to grow. Growing is never easy and any parent would know, I imagine, that you can't protect your child from anything or from everything that is going to hurt it. If you try to do that, then you don't allow them to live.

In order to prevent a child from falling and hurting itself, you would have to prevent it from standing up in the first place, which is not allowing it to be a human being. So, up to a point, there is the element of God looking on while we hurt each other and it must hurt God more than it hurts us . . . No, can we scrap that bit? It sounds awful, like a sort of non-interference policy, and I think it is more than that.

A lot of it has to do with the fact that I no longer see God as an 'out there' being who has got complete control of it and can step in and make everything right and wave a magic wand. The power of God is there to equal the love of God but, a bit like I said earlier, our way of experiencing the love of God is through people, and, if we are going to be agents of God's love, then we have also got to be agents of God's power and we are not very good at that.

We are putting the brakes on and not allowing that love and power to reach out to the suffering world through us. We see injustice and we don't act. It is by our growing in love that we can at least help the question of suffering. I don't see it being solved altogether in the next three years or something but it is a process. If God really loves, he(she) will not step in and lay down the law because love is allowing us to be who we are and not to be puppets. Something like that.

I hope to have a ministry outside the established Church because I think there is a spiritual hunger that is not being met anywhere. I have no idea what form that would take. I certainly don't see myself as a 'spiritual director'. At the moment I have a strong desire to work with young teenagers, although I have no experience, no training and nothing to recommend me to that sphere at all. I just know that it is something that I get very excited about when it comes up in conversation. I would like to give it a try. I'd be happy to do any other work in the community unless they made me the housekeeper or put me in the kitchen.

Poverty, Celibacy and Obedience

Poverty is hard to get used to. Looking at me, nobody would suggest that I was poor. I live in a large house with a beautiful garden in an extremely wealthy area and I always have enough to eat and enough to wear and I don't have to worry about the rates or the mortgage or whatever. So poverty is a difficult term to use now for people in a religious community because it doesn't mean the same as it did in the past, and it certainly doesn't mean for us the same as it would mean for the person on the street. Many of the people I work with have an experience of poverty that is much much deeper than mine.

For me it goes as far as not having my own money and not having my own possessions. That doesn't mean that it isn't hard to get used to, when you have had eleven years of earning a salary and being able to do more or less what you like with that money.

As I said earlier, I used to have great holidays. And I like expensive clothes. I was never extravagant, but it was nice to have enough not to worry. Now any money that I have is not mine but communal money, so I have to think very carefully before I buy anything, say from an Oxfam shop, and be sure that I really need it.

It is the lack of choice that is the hardest thing. The word 'poverty' doesn't really explain what it means very well. It makes sense and it is something that you have to learn to live with. But I'd probably have found it the same had I chosen marriage and children because I wouldn't have wanted to work if I was a parent and we would be struggling on one salary with a mortgage and there would not have been enough money for things like going to Mexico. So in one sense it is not that much different from other people's experience.

★ ★ ★

Chastity, er, yes, what is there to say about that? I didn't have a sexual relationship with any of my boyfriends. I didn't want to without being married, but I did have a couple of very important relationships.

Obviously the idea of being a nun got in the way. There was one man who wanted to marry me and I wanted to marry him – very much – but I couldn't give him an answer while I was still not sure about this. And I was adamant about not wanting to keep him hanging on because I don't think that is fair. So I chose to break off the relationship because I couldn't give him any promise. I don't believe in having that kind of a relationship just for the sake of it. I needed to feel that he was free to form a deep relationship with someone else, which he wouldn't have been if I had still been around. So I broke it off.

It wasn't that I didn't want to have sex with him, but I guess I've always been fairly conventional, having been taught that it 'wasn't right'. Not necessarily that I believe that for other people, but for me I don't think it would have been right because of where I was at the time in terms of teaching and belief. I don't know how I would react in that situation now. I certainly would never say to anyone else, 'This is wrong', but how I would react in the same situation I don't know. As far as other people are concerned, I think there is a lot more to it than hard and fast rules. I suppose I would say that there would have to be commitment to the other person of some kind but not necessarily permanent commitment, and that there would have to be mutual respect and self-respect on both sides, but not necessarily marriage.

I can remember being very persuasively argued with by a Muslim in Kenya who said, 'Marry me' and I said, 'No I can't marry you because you are a Muslim and I'm a Christian and I don't believe in mixed marriages because you argue about religion all the time.' And we argued about who was going to convert.

The idea of celibacy is something that you have to work at. It doesn't come easily. And how do you do that? I guess just by keeping going and not walking out. And by understanding who you are. I think that it's to do with understanding rather than denying. Accepting the fact that, yes, you are a human being, a woman. And not denying that.

As far as the vow is concerned, it is the finality of it. To say 'This is something that is denied to me for ever.' And for me, I don't really know what I am denying myself. There is no way of knowing if that makes it harder because each individual reacts differently. In anything that you decide in life there is always 'What would have happened if . . . ?' And there is no way of knowing.

As far as I'm concerned, celibacy is something that I feel relatively comfortable with. It isn't something that I find to be a huge problem. I wouldn't go so far as to say it's no problem but it isn't a major problem. I'd be extremely grateful if it stays that way.

★ ★ ★

Obedience is my favourite one. I'm really good on obedience. When it suits me. Obedience is something that we tend to associate with children more, or dogs even, than with adults. I think in the world today obedience is a negative word as far as adults are concerned. It's not actually a negative concept when you think it through. It's about living as a group, living as community, as opposed to living as an individual, but being an individual within the group.

I think it is important that people realise that it is informed obedience, that you are aware of why you are doing something. And it's a lot about trust. Somebody asks you to do something and if for any reason they don't give you a reason why, then you have to trust them. But that doesn't happen often.

When I joined this community, I knew that six months of my novitiate would be spent in another house. It was known that I didn't want to go to Bristol and the only other options at the time were Canada or Australia. I was asked casually 'If you had the choice where would you choose?' and I said 'Canada'. But whether that had any bearing on the decision to send me to Canada for six months I don't know. You have to trust that they know what they are doing.

I would never had said this three years ago, but the timetable is restrictive in terms of what you do when. Not that I'd do anything different, I would just do it at different times. And a little bit more free time would make it easier, I think. Or maybe it wouldn't.

What I most love about the life here is the freedom. It sounds weird because I was just moaning about the restrictions and the timetable and stuff, but at the same time community has allowed me to be free to be who I am. I don't have to pretend. You can't quite get away with this outside, not pretend and hold down a job as well.

You have total freedom here to be different. Nobody passes judgment on you. It isn't as if I ever experienced any kind of persecution, but I always felt a certain pressure to conform to whatever group I was in at the time – but it's not like that here. I'm allowed to conform to a non-conformist group. It's very freeing. You have the support of the people around you to stand out against values that you believe to be false. That isn't to say that everyone in this community holds the same set of values, but somehow being a sister and occasionally wearing a habit gives you freedom. Freedom to say things that you couldn't say otherwise. You can challenge people. For example, there was a conference recently and there was a conversation about why people go to church and I felt that being a sister I could express views that were different and they were still taken seriously. You can be as different as you choose, if you are a sister.

I couldn't have joined a community that wore a habit. We wear them here for special occasions, but that is all. I could just see myself swanning around in a long habit but it would have been play-acting. It didn't seem real, and I wanted more reality. I looked at several communities and chose this one just because it felt right. I don't normally base decisions on my heart rather than my head but somehow on this occasion it seemed important. Everyone said, 'Why don't you go and join the sisters at Wantage?' So I didn't. So far I've been a novice for two and a half years, and I have to be a novice for at least three years up to four years. Then I have to ask if I can be a junior sister for at least three years up to six years. So there are seven and a half years before I can ask to make life vows, so I've got lots of time to think!

My parents find it a bit hard because they had always thought that I would be a wife and mother. But, once they got over the shock, they have been very supportive. My brothers thought I was crazy, but they were quite interested. Actually I've never met anything but support from anybody. My friends were extremely supportive. They couldn't understand it but they still stood by me. My boss was amused. It was difficult telling my boyfriend at the time. I remember sitting in the pub thinking, 'How am I going to say this?' I think he wanted the relationship to end in marriage but he had to accept that it wasn't going to. He said, 'You're going to be a nun, aren't you?' It sounds so absurd doesn't it?

And it's been tough. The one thing that I want is to grow. To grow towards God, whatever that means. There have been times when I've wanted to walk out and I'm sure there will be again. But I've never wanted the kind of life where I hide from everything that's difficult.

Life here is so rich. I'm a much more alive person here than I ever was before. And I've been pretty alive. How alive you are is how much you experience of what life is, what life sends you. You can either experience everything second-hand from TV, books, and other people or you can go out and live it. I think most people do a combination of the two. But in a life like this there is no way of hiding from everything that life throws at you. (Or there may be, but I haven't discovered it yet.) Everybody gets thrown at them a certain amount of joy, pleasure, pain, frustration. Everybody experiences all those things and some people are better than others at hiding from them. Even pleasure can be something that you hide from because the losing of it is too painful. In this life there aren't so many places to hide, and so I live life much more fully. And I experience more different aspects of life than I ever did before in my comfortable house with my friends and my secure job.

It's much more exciting. That's why it's hard. But that's why it's worth it.

Since this interview Lynn has begun a four-year diploma course in genealogy

'Family Trees and stuff . . . because we used to run children's homes and there are a lot of people now that come to us because they want

to find their relatives. I'm now working mainly in the archive library as well as the chapel and the kitchen . . . It is hard here. Some of it I enjoy and some of it I don't!'

Lynn has now taken vows for three to six years which will enable her to take life vows any time after that . . .

sister julie

I met this bloke on the train yesterday and he said, 'Are you Roman Catholic?' and I said 'No, I'm Anglican' and he said maybe he could tell me his joke anyway. He'd tried it on two bishops and a Catholic sister. So I waited. He asked, 'What do you call a Sister who goes to be a hermit in a washing machine?' And the answer is Systematic, er, Sister-matic. Terrible isn't it? These are the dubious advantages of taking public transport in a habit.

sister Julie

COMMUNITY OF THE HOLY NAME

DERBY, ENGLAND

Sister Julie is thirty-eight and has been in her Derby community for two years. At the time of this interview Sister Julie was based at the community's Chester house where she will stay for a further seven months. The CHN sisters live a mixed life combining prayer with ministry in the local community. They wear a traditional habit but Julie doesn't have to wear her veil all the time, so she doesn't. We had a fun interview and both laughed a lot; I remember her laughter and the more than generous amounts of cakes and biscuits that were served.

There are now about sixty sisters in Britain in this community and a similar number in South Africa, Lesotho and Zululand. In this country we have the main house in Derby, then there is this house, a house in Keswick, and two in Nottingham. We also have two sisters who work at Lambeth Palace, and a house at Oakham. Over in South Africa they are all now Basotho, Zulu or Swazi sisters, whereas here we are all white, so it is very good when they come to work with us or we with them.

We have five hermit sisters who live on their own. Hermit sisters live a solitary life and bring the needs of the world to God in prayer. They live the community life first and then they may feel that God is calling them to live exclusively as a solitary. They live partly supported by the community and partly supported by craftwork that they do. One lives in a caravan, and some work on icons or calligraphy. It is a very unusual calling. Of course Sister Wendy Beckett is a solitary, but has become widely known because of her work. I'm not sure which community she is attached to. But I don't know a lot about the life of solitaries, as of course we don't tend to meet them!

My parents both went to church, so from the age of about six I remember being bored and flicking through the Book of Common Prayer and finding prayers for rain and burial at sea. I think it gave me a crazy picture of all sorts of things. I remember Sunday school in the church hall and stories about Jesus, and I liked those. I was confirmed quite early, at eleven, and it's interesting what I remember from my confirmation classes – that Henry VIII started the Church of England and why different colour vestments are worn in different seasons. Before the confirmation we were interviewed one by one and the curate asked me what I wanted to do when I grew up and I said I'd like to be a teacher. He asked me, 'Do you think that is what God wants you to do?' And I was surprised to think that God might have something to do with the rest of life and not just on Sundays. And that was confirmation.

Then I started helping in the Sunday school and helping with the little ones and finally I joined the choir. The choir was well run and we all sang parts and so it was musically interesting and kept me there. Meanwhile I moved into the top stream at the secondary modern school and at thirteen I was transferred to a grammar school where I stayed until I was eighteen and went to teacher training college. The whole group of us stayed in the choir at church all this time, the social scene was good and I loved the music.

Of course, at secondary school, in religious education I had to pretend that I didn't know the answers. I'd already made the mistake at school of admitting publicly to liking classical music. We had a new music teacher and he went around the class asking what groups or musicians we liked. I was hooked at the time on Mendelssohn's *Fingal's Cave* and I made the mistake of being honest and saying so. He said 'A lone pebble on the beach'. And I thought, 'Oops, that was a mistake.' So I certainly wasn't going to admit at school to knowing anything about the Bible.

I did have friends but I was a shy child and very studious and I worked hard. I learned to play the piano and practised my way up the grades and I was really happier studying and playing my classical music than at the local disco. I think I found all that quite frightening. Up until the age of fifteen I wanted to teach Latin, at the risk of alienating nine-tenths of the readership! Latin – I know, it's terrible isn't it? I liked finding the roots of words and finding the patterns to them, but when I discovered that to do Latin you also had to take Greek and ancient history too, I changed my mind. I applied to do music at teacher training college but I found that, although I played the piano, I was lost as I had no foundations in harmony and theory. So I transferred to English and just kept up music as a hobby. I went on to do an M.Ed. in Music in Education later.

In 1981 teaching jobs were hard to come by but I got one in Rotherham where I worked for five years. After that I got a job teaching music in middle school and I was about to apply for deputy headships, when I felt that this wasn't enough – and that was the beginning of what led me to where I am now.

My experiences with God had been, initially as a teenager, to do with the wonder of creation. I was aware of God in the infinite space, the sky, the setting sun. Then later, when I used to play the organ on my own in the church, I was often very reluctant to leave the church. I can only describe the feeling in the sanctuary area as a tremendous feeling of love and attraction holding on to me. And a sense of joy, an energy and a presence really that came out of the church with me and stayed on the way home.

Of course I wondered as a teenager whether God was really there. But I'd walk down the street saying to God, 'Well, if you're not really there then I'm talking to nobody and this is all a bit ridiculous.' I had been bought a picture of *The Light of the World* by Holman Hunt on the theme of asking God to come into your life. I did that as a teenager, so I did go to church because I had chosen God for myself and because I wanted to, rather than because it was something that my parents wanted. I think I chose because of this feeling of love.

When I was older I changed churches so that I could be my own person rather than just my parents' daughter. I used to go up to my room on Sunday afternoons. Sometimes I'd just daydream and stare out of the window or be reading – sometimes my Bible but often nothing specifically connected with God at all . . . and there was this feeling of being loved again. I remember the same sense of love and a feeling of joy . . . such a tremendous sense of love that I cried sometimes. It felt as if I could throw open the window and fly. I didn't try it but that was the feeling, it was marvellous. I knew God was real.

So after those heightened awareness experiences there was often a dreadful awful clatter as I came down to earth again. I remember I'd go to evening service to play the organ, and then when I came home and it would be so lonely that I'd think I had got it all wrong. It was then that I'd think that I should have been looking for someone to be with because I couldn't stand the awful loneliness. By the time I was twenty-five I was beginning to be overwhelmed by the expectations of my parents, my friends, and society in general. They all seemed to want me to find a partner and get married.

Meanwhile I'd been involved in the local church doing loads of jobs. The organist left and they asked if I'd take over temporarily. I played temporarily for eight years and eventually went to the vicar and said that I needed more time to pray. I was doing far too much and I started to be aware of it. There was a TV drama called *Brides of*

Christ, an Australian drama, and the first episode showed a young girl leaving her fiancé, and joining a community, and it hit me like a ton of bricks. I thought, 'That is what I should be doing.'

It was absurd, and I said to myself, 'Don't be ridiculous.' I didn't know anything about the Religious Life and I told myself I was being crazy. But it didn't go away – I thought, 'It can't be this, so maybe it's a call for ordination.' That seemed far more reasonable, so I made moves towards that and thought at the same time I'd read some books about the Anglican Religious Life – only to find that at that time there weren't any. When I went to see the Director of Women's Ministry she said, 'Have you ever considered the Religious Life?' I think I said, 'Er, well actually there is a lot of that in me.' Or something stupid like that.

Anyway I had a series of appointments with her to discuss ordination, and between times I read a lot of books. It was a bit as if I was trying to push myself into the ordained ministry to avoid the Religious Life. Anyway I'd been praying and asking God to show me which it was. I went off on holiday saying to God, 'I just don't know what is going on here, but if this is what you want me to do, you had better tell me a bit more about it and I'll do it.'

That is something that I found all along: you have to make the jump and say, 'Yes', when you don't know all the facts, and only then do things become clearer. I knew nothing about this life at that stage, but I felt so strongly that that was what God was pushing at, I said, 'Well, OK, if that is what you want I'll not run away from it any longer and I'll not try and turn it into a call for ordination or something else'. That was a Saturday.

So I went on this walking holiday as I'd planned and on the Sunday there was a walk arranged. I wanted to go to church so I thought I'd go early in the morning at eight before the walk – but I overslept. Rather than go on the walk and miss the service I decided to walk alone and drive to a service. I walked into the church and there was a nun sitting in the congregation. It was a shock because you don't often see sisters around do you, in ordinary places? I'd never seen a sister in real life before. Most of the communities in Britain are in the South of England and I'd always lived in the North.

After the service I approached her. She was a sister from the Community of the Holy Name. She took me across to see the house in Keswick and I sat down and explained what I'd been through for the last nine months since seeing this television programme and asked what I should do next.

She gave me the address of the council of Anglican communities and suggested that I visited a couple of communities and keep reading and praying. A lot of people say you visit a number of communities and one just feels like home. They are all different. It was very strange talking to her, I was more and more convinced myself that I was on the right track and I was beginning to think, 'How am I going to tell everyone?'

I did read one book. It is quite an old book, with the stories of eight people's calling to the Religious Life. It was edited by Maria Boulding and called *A Touch of God*. When I read the story, although the details were all very old and communities have changed a lot since then, something in Maria Boulding's own story touched me at a very deep level.

My call was like . . . er, well . . . how can I describe it? First of all there was a restlessness with teaching which I couldn't understand. I thought at first it was just because of all the changes in the National Curriculum, but it wasn't that. I was still enjoying it, I loved the children and I was about to get promotion. There was just a restlessness. And there was a feeling that I didn't want to be so busy in the church. I felt good at school because I was doing something worthwhile, and I was fine at church because I was doing something worthwhile and I enjoyed my time with my friends outside – but life felt too fragmented and split up.

When I read about this life, about the rhythm of the day, for example, it just seemed, instead of this fragmentation, to all be coming from the same point. So the call for me contained this feeling, wanting life to be all joined together instead of all split up into little bits. It was also wanting to have more time for God in a direct way.

Also there was a feeling that if you weren't part of a couple then you were battling against the tide of the world. Everywhere you went you needed a partner to be able to join in with things. It was difficult to be able to keep up with that. I didn't feel, I don't think, that if I hadn't got a partner then I was no good and I couldn't join in with life, but it was an expectation and I didn't feel that I wanted to go along with that expectation.

This call wasn't rejecting that, it wasn't, 'Well, I'm no good at this, so I'll do that.' But it was a relief that I didn't have to go towards that expectation any longer. I always wanted to get married, but not to have children – which is amazing because I love children and I've loved teaching. It always seemed strange to me that I didn't feel I wanted to have my own children. I think it was something to do with time being all split up and the fact that children take up so much time, but it wasn't from a selfish point of view because I gave them all this time in the classroom – but I always felt there was something else. This drawing towards the Religious Life made sense of it.

This is all very difficult to describe and find words for. The calling also made sense of a feeling I'd had of being a bit different, of going against the normal expectations of the world. Suddenly it wasn't weird, here were other people who were doing the same thing! The answer to why they were doing it was because God wanted it, basically. Once I'd got a little further along and visited a number of communities and decided that, yes, God was calling me to the Religious Life, the relief of that was absolutely amazing. Friends at school said, 'What on earth has happened to you? You look totally different.'

I had had a feeling of strain that I was trying to hold things together. I had to join in with the competition for promotion, all the busy-ness, and the expectations of society that you'd have a busy social life, and suddenly I didn't have to keep up with all that any longer. I was being torn in all these different directions and I felt, for the first time, that all my energy could go in one direction and tied in with the experiences I had had with God earlier on.

So I wrote and got a booklet listing the different communities and picked out three; Burford Priory, Freeland (which is the contemplative community of St Clare) and here. Burford is a mixed community of monks and nuns, but the novitiate has been closed to women for about twelve years – actually they have just opened the community to new women again but at that time it was closed. And the community at Freeland is contemplative which obviously wasn't me. So after visiting these two I decided that God was definitely not calling me to community. I had obviously got the wrong end of the stick altogether and perhaps I should look at the ordination track again. I immediately rang the new Director of Ordinands to make an appointment with her. But I decided to keep my Derby appointment anyway, just for a quiet weekend off to recover from it all.

When I got out of the car at the Derby cottage and looked across to where the main building was, I thought that it looked like a cross between the halls of residence where I had enjoyed being at college and the house where I was living at that moment. For a start it was modern, unlike the other two buildings I'd visited, and I liked that immediately. The guest sister who settled me in was really welcoming and she introduced me immediately to the sister who was the novice guardian at the time. She knew that I had been considering becoming a sister and said, in a very relaxed way that, if I wanted to, I could chat the following day.

I went into the chapel that night for the quarter of an hour's silence before the evening service. I was thinking that it was all very nice and they were all very lovely but I'd done with all this idea of joining a community. After about five minutes this awful feeling crept over me and I thought, 'God's asking me to come here.' It was as clear as that.

At that stage I still couldn't be sure that it wasn't just a crazy thought in my head. I only had the strength of feeling and conviction inside myself to be guided by. I knew that it had to be tested. So I went to bed and wandered around the place the next day feeling tremendously excited and apprehensive as well. I talked to the novice guardian and the superior the next day. I don't know what it was about this community really. It seemed so open and friendly and there was a lot going on. There were about thirty sisters there at the time and two novices.

Anyway, I booked to visit the community again a couple of months later and went back to my job. My biggest problem at that stage was the fact that I just couldn't face telling my mum that this was what I was going to do. So in that two months in-between period I tried very hard to convince myself that God wanted me to be ordained to the priesthood. I had an appointment fixed with the Director of Ordinands, but I went back to the Community of the Holy Name the weekend before I was supposed to see her and in that second weekend any doubts that I had were taken away.

It didn't come easily. I remember on the Saturday morning . . . I had asked for a couple of Bible passages to think through for the couple of days I was there . . . and I was wrestling with the two and thinking, 'Is it the Religious Life? Is it ordination? How the heck do I tell which it is?' I went to talk to one of the sisters and asked, 'How did you feel about it and did you ever think that you'd got it wrong?' She couldn't make my mind up for me but by the end of the weekend it was just a very strong feeling inside. That is a difficult thing to understand and it's difficult for me to explain better than that.

At one stage, something that I did do – I read this in Gerry Hughes's book, *God of Surprises* – he talks about how you discern what God is asking you to do and what you are making up and projecting yourself. He says – it is so obvious really – write a list of reasons for and against course of action 'A' and for and against course of action 'B' and then pray through that. If you feel peaceful with one particular list then that is as good an indication as you can get, really. Whereas if you feel torn two ways, that may not be the right option. I felt peaceful in the decision, and energised by it. It was as if it was a path to wholeness. It was that same joy that I'd felt when I walked back from church. My awareness of the presence of God had been quashed for a long time by my trying to keep up with my expectations and society's expectations about what my life should be. And then suddenly here was a way that my experience of God could be joined up again. I could be free to be myself in a more complete way, a more directed way.

I came back for a third weekend and asked them if I could live alongside the community for a ten-day period during a half term from school. After this ten days I was sure that it was the right thing to do but I waited another year to join. I did this for two reasons; I wanted to finish my teaching career properly, to give the school time to sort things out and to finish with the class. Also my father died suddenly and I wondered if I should stay with my mother for a while. I wanted to spend a lot of time with her in the first year after my father's death. I had been living only five minutes away from where she lived, so I gave her a long time to get used to the idea before I went. It was difficult telling her because she was very, very against it. It wasn't that she expected me to stay with her – it was just that she knew nothing about the Religious Life and thought that all the old stories of oppression were true. I think she hoped that I would get over it if it wasn't mentioned, and for a while I felt very guilty. As it happens, she sees me quite a bit, because she can visit whenever she wants and I visit her a lot. I don't know about all the other communities, but certainly in this one your own family is as much a part of you as the community is. And I'm still the same person, despite the funny clothes, and when we are on holiday we don't have to wear the funny clothes, and we pass as quite normal!

One of the stories in this book *A Touch of God* – I don't know what the date of this book was – but it was a story of this woman spreading out her towel on the floor with a metal basin and a pitcher of water to have her weekly wash. I was thinking, 'Could I put up with that?' I remember I wrote a list at one stage of things that I thought I just couldn't put up with, and either they would have to change or God would have to do some marvellous work to change me. I remember deciding that I would definitely not go anywhere that didn't have a bath! I was just asking myself, 'How much hardship am I prepared to put up with, and how much of this is just old-fashioned and out-dated and ridiculous?' But I did of course find that, firstly, all communities have baths and, secondly, that you can have a bath whenever you want.

I do think that I was called here. I think that an ability to hear calling is to do with developing listening skills and discriminating between different sounds. I think through life our main calling is to be ourselves and to become more yourself and that there are different choices about the ways that you can do that. The choices include whether you are going to marry or live with a partner, or whether you are going to be single. Your choice of career . . . well, who is listening for God to be speaking? And I think you can hear God's voice in a lot of different ways. It took me a long time to realise that God works most of all through common sense – that was a complete revelation to me I think. God doesn't usually ask things that are totally ridiculous.

I heard a story about a lady who used to get up in the morning and she used to listen very carefully. If she felt that God was telling her to put on her left stocking, she'd put on her left stocking and if she couldn't hear God telling her to put on her right stocking then she spent the day with one stocking on. We would not advise listening in that way! Add a large dose of common sense in all things.

And then there is listening to who you truly are inside yourself. So for me, the way that I felt fragmented, and then that things were coming together, meant a lot to me. I wrote to a friend when I came that I felt I could be myself here, but more so. And I think that is God's call – to be ourselves, only more so. That 'more so' bit is the bit that he draws out and that is the result of his calling. So how do you know that it is not just something that you have created for yourself? Well, if it works, if it makes me able to love God more and love other people more, then that is answering God's call. I feel that, even after two years, that I can do that best in this way of life. There are always more choices within the choices. Like one of those many-coloured balls that you have in a dance hall that reflects our many different colours, we are becoming more clear about what kind of light we are reflecting back to God. And I think that it is something to do with freedom as well. In order to play a game of football, and to be free to be creative within it, the players have to have boundaries on the pitch and a set of rules and so on. If I'm a goal-keeper, I can't score goals. I think that is a bit of an analogy, not a very good one really, but by following up what you feel is your calling you make a choice between following different sets of rules.

I think when you are trying to find out what your calling is you need to start by looking at who you are. One thing I found helpful was looking back to junior school, to a time before you had any particular responsibilities, and looking at what energised you then and what you most enjoyed doing, and that helps you find bits of yourself which, because of later responsibilities, you lose – the different sides of creativity or things to do with play which have been made serious and which as an adult you may not do any more.

Christ said, 'My purpose is to do the will of the one who sent me.' And I think that is what we are all trying to do – to do God's will; at any rate, anybody who says the Lord's prayer says, 'Thy will be done.' The difficult bit sometimes is understanding what is being said to you by the circumstances that surround you; I understand them through prayer. Putting myself in front of God and listening to what God is saying through my heart and through reading Scripture. Which set of circumstances energised me and which took my energy? Which things was I good at and which wasn't I good at? Also the Bible says that Christ was made obedient through suffering and – back to my interest in words – when you look up 'suffer' it actually means 'to bear underneath'. So we are bearing underneath the circumstances which are there and I think there is an element of waiting for the bits to fall into place so that you can see where to go next.

There are no black and white answers to discerning what God wants for you. All you can do is get all the information you can, and open yourself to God in prayer. If we look at the life of Christ, the circumstances weren't brilliant for him all the time and he certainly had to use his common sense and work within the situation that he was in, but one day he had to get up out of his carpentry shop and decide that he was not called to be a carpenter.

Prayer itself is not black and white. The first thing that I'd always say when I talk about prayer is that I'm never sure whether I'm praying or not. There are a lot of books on prayer speaking of many systems that people have worked out, and people read them and think, 'Oh well, I haven't been doing any of this, therefore I haven't been praying.' But that isn't so. Prayer is a relationship. Sometimes in a relationship you are going to talk and sometimes you are going to be quiet and just be with each other. Sometimes you will talk about superficial everyday things and once in a while you will hit on something that is really really important and has repercussions for years to come.

Christ said, 'Live in me as I do in you.' So prayer is just talking to God, listening to God and being with God, and that will then lead us to each other. It leads to an openness of relationship with one another, to a place where we are not competitive with one another and can admit that we are vulnerable and are not trying to be possessive. Prayer leads you to see everything in life as God's gift so that our relationships with one another are a gift rather than something that we've got a right to. It directly affects the way we relate to others. You can't separate prayer and life. It is all the same. It is simply that when we think about a certain way of relating to God then we call it prayer. We bring to God what we are and the sum total of our lives so far and our hopes for the future and all the rest of us. We can then be changed by being opened up to God's transforming power. When people don't pray, perhaps it is because we are afraid of change. Not that God won't answer our prayers but that he will. Prayer is dangerous because of what God might ask of us.

I can't do a lot by myself but with God I can. On the face of it, it seems ludicrous that God should ask us to pray. I mean if God can do anything anyway, why ask human beings to pray? But he does ask us to, he asks us to co-operate with him in making the world unfold and be transformed. We are called to be creators with God.

The difference between living in the convent and living outside is that in the convent I am loved for who I am, rather than for what I can do or achieve. The community has enabled a shift in my knowledge of God from knowledge in my head to knowledge in my heart and that affects the way I relate to other people. It has taught me that God accepts me as I am. Before I came to community I could have told you what the Christian faith was – but I hadn't really experienced it. I wasn't secure enough in myself not to try and win approval by what I did rather than who I was. It has been like coming home – coming home as an adult rather than coming home as a child. I wish I could describe it better. Home is more being with people, rather than a physical place – and then it is even wider than that. Home is the wider Christian family and the human family in total. If home is where the people that you love are, the more people you love the bigger your home becomes. When you are frightened of approaching people just as you are, frightened that they'll reject you, then you are enclosing yourself. So, now that I've learned that I don't have to work at driving myself along and trying to win approval, I can make mistakes and say sorry and get up and start again. Being accepted and loved by community has helped me to understand that I'm accepted and loved by God. So life, instead of being a survival course, is now an adventure.

Poverty, Celibacy and Obedience

Poverty. It is tempting to see poverty purely in the spiritual terms of being dependent on God. It is obviously not about abject poverty but about looking after the world's resources. There is the constant question of whether you need 'things' or whether you are trying to use them as a security. That is about as far as I've got with it so far, but each time I read through the writings about the vows I find something fresh in them.

I bought a large terraced house when I was twenty-seven that was cheap at the time, just before the prices went up. And I sold it later for a two-bedroomed semi-detached house which I loved. Two months after buying the second house I realised that I was about to explore the Religious Life. That was one of the hardest things initially. I thought that it couldn't be right because I had just bought this house. I sold everything or gave things away – house, car, possessions, cats, the whole lot went. The practical and physical side of getting rid of the stuff was harder than the idea of it and it was a relief when the stuff was gone. I've always been a fairly uncluttered person but some of the stuff was hard to part with. It has been a case of getting rid of it all a bit at a time. I miss the house. It was strange, the first week I was here the dustbin lorry came round. I was really upset by the dustbin lorry coming round because I realised that I didn't have a dustbin of my own any more, let alone a house of my own. I could have rented the house out until I took life vows but I decided to sell it and to put the money into unit trusts to be kept secure.

I miss my CD player most because I'm a classical music lover. I miss my organ music, but while working at this house I sing with the nave choir in the cathedral, so it is almost as if things have been taken away with one hand and given back with the other. They all march in wearing their cassocks and I wear my habit. It would be a bit hot to sing in both with one on top of the other. Apart from that, I still have my Walkman and a number of my CDs so I'm hardly living a life of deprivation.

★ ★ ★

Celibacy. I did have relationships; my first serious boyfriend was when I was seventeen. That one lasted for about six months and I remember I was devastated when it ended. He decided that something was missing in the relationship, but I remember I got over it by the time I went to college. Then I had another relationship when I was at college, but that one ended when we both got jobs at opposite ends of the country. We had a brilliant time together, but it wasn't enough for either of us to give up careers for. We are great friends and actually we are still in touch.

Then there was no one for a long long time. The next man I met who I fancied like mad was a man that I'd taught with in my first year of teaching and really liked, but I thought he wasn't interested in me other than being friendly as a fellow teacher. Anyway he suddenly rang up and said, 'I've got some computer programmes that I think you might like.' I thought, 'Strange, this is an interesting opening line.' But he eventually got around to, 'Would you like to go to the pictures tomorrow night?' And I said, 'Yes, I would, I'd be delighted.' We had a lovely evening and it was fairly obvious that he was going to ask me out again. The problem was that by this time I was considering joining community and I was desperately thinking how to casually say, 'Er, there is something I've got to tell you . . .'

There is no casual way to tell a man that you are joining a convent. But he listened and went on asking me out anyway and we had a really good time for the next six months. He was hoping that I'd decide that the convent wasn't for me. I liked him very much and we got on really well, and even though he was someone that I'd fancied for years and now he was interested in me, I had decided by this time that the community was for me. Having him waiting, quite literally, as he came to pick me up after the ten-day visit, was not enough to change my mind. I'm fairly confident that we'd have married if I'd not chosen to come to community. But having that relationship was very helpful for me because I feel that I came here with my eyes open, knowing what I was choosing.

What is so wonderful about being here is that it frees up your relationship with men in some ways. There is nothing going on which means that every time you are having a meaningful conversation with a man there is no question about whether it might lead on to a relationship. You can just approach more people as yourself and they can approach you as themselves; there is no hidden agenda. Also there is no need for a meaningful relationship with a man to become something else or to come to an abrupt end because it is not becoming something else. There isn't an ambiguity all the time, there is a freedom.

After I'd been at the convent for a little while, I remember going to the novice guardian and saying, 'I don't think I want to be celibate.' And she smiled and said, 'No, none of us do.' I think it is very difficult because it is very lonely. It's fine to have open, free, and unambiguous relationships with a lot of people, but the natural human instinct is to want to have close and intimate relationships with just one person. But the celibacy is a necessary part of this life and I suppose we accept it as part of the calling. I mean it's not as if we don't have close friendships in community. I know you hear these stories about the old days when nuns weren't allowed to talk to each other about themselves or become emotionally close to each other but of course it isn't like that any more. Compared to a lot of the human race who are lonely we certainly have a lot more companionship than many. And of course many people are lonely within marriage.

Celibacy isn't an area that I've really worked through very fully yet. I think that with all the vows your understanding of them grows over the years, and this is one that I've only just begun to understand little glimmers of. But I wouldn't cross it off the list if I got the chance – I think it is important. It is a way of saying to God that I give the whole of myself, and I'll try and respond to whatever I feel God is asking me to do in different circumstances. I'm free to do that, whereas if I was attached to one person I wouldn't have the same freedom to respond to God's calling.

Part of sexuality is the creativity, the Old Testament idea of sharing in the handing on of life, the life force. If you are not in a sexual relationship you are still creative in your expression of yourself, in your relationships, in your worship, in your being. Something I'd love to do – I haven't had the chance to do any yet but I think I will – is to do some dance to express this. I'm more happy with my sexuality here than I ever was outside because again there was that ambiguity about how things are going to be interpreted. Here, when you are in a habit, you are making a statement that the sexual side of things is not an option. Does this make any sense? It's about putting the whole of yourself into what you are doing. I don't think you are ignoring your sexuality in this life, you are just choosing not to express it in one particular way.

We read that celibacy is a gift – I find that hard to swallow. There are occasions when you'd like to have a physical relationship with someone, and it's a case of acknowledging that you feel like that and then saying to God, 'This is how I feel and I'm not very happy about this but I still believe that this is the way you want me to live my life.' It's important to be honest and open and ask God to take the feelings of frustration and disgruntlement and do something useful with them. I offer God my feelings in a similar way if I get angry about something. I say, 'I don't want to feel like this so please take this and do something with it.' That way you've not ignored the feeling or repressed it but you've acknowledged it and handed it over to God. 'Sacrifice' is a really dirty word these days but I think it is a sacrifice, an offering to God. It doesn't stop us being affectionate, or mean that you can't give or receive a hug if you need one.

★ ★ ★

Obedience. Well there is a part of me that says, 'I'm not doing this one, I'm not going to be obedient to anybody.' What I said before about listening to God – the root meaning of 'obedience' is to 'hear towards' – so again you are trying to hear towards what God is asking. You may need to wait until you can hear clearly, so you may be asked by the community to do something that you don't feel happy with, but you do it anyway and wait for the meaning of it to become clear later on. We try and work with one another in a way which is going to bring out the best in each other. It is a reflection of trusting God. In some of the circumstances of life you just can't see where something is leading or see what possible good can come out of what you are experiencing, but if you wait then you begin to see that there was some sense in it all the way along.

In community, people aren't asked to do things that they will find difficult because it's realised they will find them difficult. Huge effort is made to make sure that we are put in situations where we'll be happy or if we have particular gifts that they are being fully used. It comes back again to trying to find out what God's will is. It is about growing in knowledge of yourself and of God through other people in community and through what you are asked to do in community.

Having been a teacher, I'm sure that the community and I will find a way to use my communication skills. I seem to have the sort of sense of humour that appeals to a seven-year-old. There are so many factors in community at the moment that are in flux; I find it best to plan life one week or one day at a time rather than think what I'm doing too far in the future. At the moment I'm leading talks for various groups, either those that come to the community here or if we are invited out to speak on various spiritual themes, and I'm finding giving those talks quite demanding enough for the present.

Of course you are sometimes asked to do things you don't want to do. I mean someone has to wash up and chop the cabbage and all the rest of it. One part of the weekly programme here is to do something artistic, some sort of craft. I've a real blind spot about craft. I just think I'm useless at all that stuff. I was asked to try some bookbinding and from the word go I just hated this bookbinding. I was determined that I was going to hate it before I even started, really. Part of it comes from a natural rebellion against doing what you are told to do, and not having control over your own life and not being able to make your own choices any more. So you take it out on the little things. Someone tried to discuss it with me in a reasonable way and I ended up storming out saying, 'This is a total waste of time, I can't see why I'm doing this!!!'

Meanwhile the other sister that I was doing the bookbinding with was over in another part of the convent and I knew that she would be there waiting for me. If I'd said, 'I'm not doing it and that's the end of it' then I would have been letting her down. So I came to the horrifying realisation that life didn't revolve entirely around me and what I wanted. So I swallowed my pride at wanting to be good at everything I did, and feeling that it was satisfying for me. Of course when I'd finally finished it I did see the value in it. It was a different sort of discipline. It was like sitting down after a long day at school and watching TV because it was mindless. In the novitiate you do so much thinking and exploring of who you are . . . and the vows and prayer and all the things we've been talking about . . . and your brain gets tired and you need to do something that just lets you switch off. That is why the suggestion had been made in the first place! But I rebelled in a childish way and almost refused to do it. It was a lot later that I saw that it wasn't a waste of time and I'm almost, but not quite, thinking that I'll ask to do some more when I go back to the house in Derby. But I don't know that I'm prepared to admit that.

What I love is living with a group of people who are all trying to give everything that they have got to God. I love the balance of the life here. There is the balance between solitude and being with other people, between times of silence and times when you are in conversation. There is the balance between when the community is by itself and when we are with other people from outside. Then there are times when we retreat and times when we are working in the outside community.

The knowledge that you are loved and accepted as you are will continue as long as you remain here. Even if you leave and find that your work is elsewhere then the love of the community will still carry on. I enjoy the freedom to experiment and make mistakes within the boundaries of community life. I feel as if I can take huge risks within it and give it everything I have without fearing that if I mess it up I'm going to lose everything. Whatever happens is a gift and God will work it in, and if you are with community things are shown up for what they really are. People aren't afraid to face reality here. And I feel I'm able to live in hope and acknowledge that, although there is a lot of darkness in the world and in us, the joy can still bubble through.

Everybody is trying to give all their time and all their abilities and all their emotions, good and bad, and all the circumstances that happen to them. It is all brought back in prayer to our relationship with God and it is all right to still be on a journey. God works with us as we are. We don't suddenly have to become good at prayer or good at anything before God can work with us and use us. The purpose is to seek God and for me it can be done more completely in community life.

Sometimes there's a knock at the door for help. Someone will say, 'Sister, my husband's left me and I don't know what to do.' That can drive you crazy. Having to be available for people all the time is hard. You can't say, 'Sorry but my day finished at five.' When you are a teacher you have the time at school for the kids and you thought you were being really generous if you worked all the way through playtime. But this is certainly not a nine-to-five job. The day starts at six-thirty in the morning and you are in your room on a good day by nine-thirty in the evening.

On the other hand – if you are not a mornings person, this is the perfect choice of life. I really love not having to talk to anyone until ten o'clock in the morning. It's absolutely wonderful!

Sister Julie is now back at the Mother house in Derby where she is in charge of the kitchen. 'If you'd have told me when I was doing microwave food for one that one day I'd be organising food for thirty every day I'm not sure I'd have believed you.' Julie is also now in charge of music at the community and is able to write music especially for the thirty sisters. 'It is new for me and a joyful challenge to be writing music with specific voices in mind. I've studied the history of the music and I really enjoy the challenge of upholding the traditional forms, the modal quality of the old plainchant, whilst expressing a contemporary vitality.'

She is also studying theology by correspondence course with St John's College, Nottingham.

Julie says: 'I'm 99 per cent sure I'll stay.'

sister margaret anne

I remember just after I was clothed as a novice I was proudly wearing my new habit and veil. The first time, quite literally, that I went out of the gate a child came along and said to his friend 'Eeergh look, she's got a funny thing on her head. What is it?' I could hardly stop and explain, 'Well, you see, it all started with St Paul . . .'

sister margaret anne

ALL SAINTS SISTERS OF THE POOR

OXFORD, ENGLAND

*I felt very at home with Margaret from first speaking to her on the
telephone. She apologised for being forty-one. Did that make her too old for
possible inclusion in my book? I replied that I was too close to forty
myself to exclude anyone for that reason.*

*What a brave interview this is. I wondered whether to use it or not.
Was I, by including this story, supporting the prejudiced view that
'people that have problems become nuns'. It would have been easier
to have chosen a simpler story – a lawyer, a dancer. But if this book
had been interviews with ten women chosen at random in the street,
one of them may have had similar or worse problems. Margaret is brave
enough to tell her story, knowing this was going into print. The media
being as it is this is no small risk on her part. If she is brave
enough to take this risk then I can follow her lead.*

Margaret is fully recovered from the difficulties of her past and 'the

experience of having been to hell' as she calls it, has given her a
sensitivity and a profound gentleness. I can see why the guests
at All Saints pour out their hearts to her.

Margaret has both a strength that inspires confidence
and a warmth that invites love.

There is a view held by some members of the general public that
'only people with psychological problems become nuns'. Then there
is another view held by some people who would like to become nuns
that 'no community would take me because I've had mental illness'.
Both views are equally untrue. What is the statistic? One in four people
have mental illness at some stage in their life? So here I am, and the
community have accepted me.

I feel that mental illness is one of society's taboos and has been a
long time. It hasn't yet been exploded and therefore people are afraid
of it. They are afraid, I think, partly because it is an unknown factor,
and partly because they think 'maybe it could happen to me.' Of
course it could happen to literally anybody. No one is totally foolproof.
No matter how much your reader might be thinking 'I'd never be
mentally ill', it's not true. We simply don't know what might happen
to us.

Also I think people are afraid because it manifests itself in such
strange forms. People become either very introverted, quiet and retiring
and can't communicate with people around them, which is the form
it took for me, or others can become aggressive.

Obviously people find the aggression scary but they are also afraid
of the introversion and find it threatening. The person in the introverted
state inhabits their own world, cut off from external reality.

The nearest analogy I can make is that it's like being in a nightmare,
except that you are awake and it's as if the cushion between the
conscious mind and the unconscious mind erupts. The unconscious,
which has all these weird archetypal images, surfaces into the conscious

mind when you are awake, and that can be very frightening for the person experiencing it.

I don't know if you've ever had the experience of having a bad dream and waking up not sure, for some seconds, what is reality and what isn't? It's like that. Like a frightening dream when you are awake and it becomes a kind of mental chaos. A disordering of your perceptions of reality. Or that is the nature of psychosis as I experienced it. I think the dictionary definition is 'a terrifying mental disturbance'.

You inhabit a different realm of reality from normal consciousness and that realm is very akin, in the form I had, to someone having a nightmare. You can imagine that things are arrayed against you – people. When you are in it, at its worst, that is reality for you. It is not anyone else's reality, that is the problem – you have lost touch with so-called objective reality. You've got your own reality which doesn't match with any other reality around you. So there is a breakdown in communication – a two-way breakdown because you can't express what you are feeling and other people can't get a handle on what is going on for you. If there is some kind of healing or therapy that happens to get you through, then you can express what is happening and get an objective view of it. Then you can get to the point when you realise that you're not well and then eventually you can get well – as I did. I've been functioning normally for about ten years now.

Very sadly, some people just keep ending up in hospital in a cyclical pattern – they don't get free of it. Some people believe it is pure chemical imbalance and reactions and you can solve it totally with drugs and there is nothing else. Well, I wouldn't go so far as to say that. I think that can be a factor, but I think there are other factors in play. If you experience tragedy as a child, as I did, then that is obviously a real factor.

My mother and father came from Ireland and my mother's name is O'Neill. She likes to think that she is descended from the Kings and Queens of Ulster. It's a joke really, but she does have good Irish blood. My father was a priest. He had been a Church of Ireland priest in

Ireland, a Protestant but don't think Ian Paisley – not that kind of 'Can't stand the Catholics' breed. My mother was brought up surrounded by Roman Catholics. It is only a minority that have the cudgel to bear. After they had my eldest brother, Hugh, they moved to a parish in the south of England where they then had their second son, Neil, and I was born five years later. I was the little sister and got very spoiled.

The tragedy struck when I was eight. My father committed suicide. In the early sixties suicide was very much a taboo subject, especially as he was a priest. I think things have moved on a lot since then but at that time it was terrible. It was all in the papers and, as you can imagine, it was terrible for my mother.

The church offered to take care of my education and I went, free of charge, to a girls' boarding school. It was a public school and I had a very good education which I enjoyed very much. But it was hard on my mother. My brothers were already away at school and I went away at ten. She'd already lost my father and then she had long stretches in term time when none of us were there. She had to work and she kept very busy. But it was hard.

There was a great leader in the church attached to the local cathedral who heard about her story and used to see her regularly – he got out his diary and just offered to support her. She was able to pour out her heart and tell him how difficult she was finding life. It was wonderful that came from someone in a leadership position in the church.

Meanwhile I loved St Margarets, Bushey, boarding school. All the things that people love about good boarding schools were true here. The staff were committed and kind and we got up to all the usual tricks. I remember boozing in the woods and getting the most innocent-looking girl to go out and get the drink so we wouldn't get caught. I was quite popular at school. They made me House Captain, not head girl I'm pleased to say, but I was head of choir as well. I got good O and A levels and went on to take English Literature at Durham University.

My year off between school and university was important. I went to South Africa to work with mentally handicapped children. That was a great learning experience. I was nineteen and it was my first experience away from home. I could have gone to lots of what were then called 'Third World' countries, and I chose South Africa because I wanted to see for myself just how bad apartheid was.

At work with the mentally handicapped children the staff were Afrikaner but they employed black African staff. I used to find it very upsetting at meal times because I couldn't eat with the black staff. I met one black African vicar, David Nkwe, who invited me to his parish in Soweto, and we processed through the streets one day into his church, singing and waving these real palms. He introduced me and I was the only white face in the congregation. It was 1975, and I had to get a permit to go and visit him.

Then I went to university, and I loved that, I lapped it up. Being able to read novels and poetry that I loved to read and then look at them in greater depth. I did do my rebellion against God and the Church but it wasn't very wild. I remember that when I was twenty I wrote home to my mother and said that I thought death was the end. I went home in the holidays but she didn't drag me out to church or anything, she let me be. So I lived my first year at Durham without any church contact. I had to make that break from the faith that had been implanted. But I didn't go that wild – I took up rowing! I remember drinking quite a lot with my friends, lager as an undergraduate and then later beer. I remember one night we had a competition as to who could drink the most gins in one night. I won.

And I did have a terrible passion for one of the lecturers. And of course he was married, and so I went through all the turmoil that creates, when you fall for someone like that. I'm afraid we didn't do anything so I can't give you a fruity story – it was just painful.

So I took up transcendental meditation (TM). I did it for about six months. My friends all said wonderful things happened to them when they were meditating, but nothing ever happened to me. I had this mantra I was given and I would repeat it day in and day out, twenty minutes silently twice a day. It's relaxing and I was interested in Eastern writings. I was searching for something, but I realised in the end that TM wasn't for me and I stopped doing it. But it was after that experience that I came to realise that 'Yes, there is a God.'

After university I went to do voluntary work in the Middle East. I went to the Gaza Strip with twelve other students and we worked and lived with the Palestinians. We were decorating pre-school play centres. It was an occupied territory – the Israelis were there with their machine guns at the ready and it was eye-opening to experience the Palestinians as an oppressed people without land and without their freedom, and living with them. I remember going into a post office one day to buy stamps and the postmaster saying to me, 'All we want is our freedom and our land.' Like the Irish situation, most people are law-abiding and just want peace.

When I was there I met a Muslim at a party and halfway through the evening he said to me, 'Excuse me, I have to go and pray now.' That made an impression on me – he wasn't showing off or anything, he just very modestly went off to go and pray. It would never occur to me if I was at a party, even now, to leave to pray. We have set times for services here but if I came to a party at your house I wouldn't go off to a side room at the time when the sisters are praying to go and pray. I just wouldn't do it.

When I got back I taught English for two years at secondary level. I loved the A level teaching but the fourteen-year-olds were too much. After two years I'd had enough. Then I took a course teaching English as a foreign language, and started doing that.

Then I had what I thought was going to be a holiday. I went to Lee Abbey, which is a holiday and conference centre in Devon run by Christians, and there I met a nun. I'd never met a nun before. She was from the Community of the Holy Name, where you've interviewed Julie. We had a few interesting, quite deep conversations and on the last day I didn't want to leave. As I stepped into the taxi I had a profound sense of God stirring me up inside. I've never had an experience like it before or since. Somehow it was an experience of God's suffering and also God's greatness all in one. It was as if God was whimpering inside me. I knew by the end of that journey that I had to go to my vicar and say that I wanted to do some kind of full-time work in the church – I didn't know what, but I knew that I wasn't going to be a teacher any more. It was just like that. It was so definite.

I didn't even know the meaning of the word 'vocation' at the time. But my vicar was wide-eyed. He could see that something had happened. He put me in touch with someone who was involved with discerning vocations but because I was going to an evangelical church the vicar didn't recommend that I became a nun. They had other suggestions, like becoming a deaconess. I then worked in a parish for a year, during which time I passed a selection to train as a deaconess. I would have done that for three years, but at the end of the first year I had an experience, which was, well it was the beginning of what became the breakdown, really, and as a result of that I didn't go back. I wasn't happy so I left the training, and eventually I had the breakdown.

I managed to hold down a job for a year in York after that, working for Age Concern. But after that I had a period of unemployment which I found very difficult, and that eventually led me to a psychiatric hospital.

From the moment I entered the hospital the psychiatrist I was under knew that there was an intimate link between my sense of abandonment by my God and my father's death. That was obviously a major factor. You don't have to have studied Freud to notice that . . . anyway I told you what it felt like earlier. It was like living in hell. But I was lucky, I came under a very good psychiatrist. I was out of hospital within a few months, still fairly vulnerable for quite a while, but it was while I was recovering that I addressed the question of my vocation again. Although I'd had a breakdown I still believed that God had called me to full-time ministry of some sort.

I was reading Isaiah one day and I had a really strong sense of myself – I don't mean a picture – nothing visual – but just a strong sense of myself, as a nun, in a habit! It took me totally by surprise. I'd never considered being a nun at all, even after having met that one at Lee Abbey. But everything suddenly began to click into place in my mind and I thought 'Yes'. My vicar who I'd spoken to years before about full-time ministry, being an evangelical, wouldn't have thought of it. It all took me totally by surprise.

I thought that if I was going to take this seriously then I'd have to do something about it. I started looking at communities. I went to the local library in York. There wasn't much to read about communities, but I found a directory of addresses and I spoke to my vicar in York and he mentioned All Saints. So I thought I'd come to Oxford and look at two of the communities at the same time, so I looked at Wantage and I looked here. Before that I'd looked at the Franciscans, where you interviewed Rose – this was about the third I'd looked at. With this one, well, on my first visit I felt at home.

One of the older sisters – she is now in the residential home – was so kind to me. She was slightly involved in the guest house – she wasn't the guest sister but she'd sit and chat to me in the evenings. She'd listen to me and I'd talk about my vocation. She was so kind, there was a special quality to her kindness. And I felt very at home in the chapel, straight away. Especially saying the Office and singing the psalms. So although I'd looked at several communities, I felt this was the one I wanted to go for.

I came knocking on their door and I said 'I'd like to join you.' I was afraid that as soon as they knew about my history and heard about mental illness they'd say 'No'. Actually, what they did was very wise. They didn't say 'No' but they didn't say 'Yes'. They said 'Wait. We want more time to elapse before you test your vocation as a nun. There should be more distance between your experience of breakdown and coming to join a community.' What they suggested was that I went to Holy Island where there is a community of lay people. It's in

Northumberland, on the coast. Much of the time it is an island, but twice a day there is a causeway linking it to the mainland.

I went up to Holy Island and did an interview and they offered me a place. So off I went. They have a retreat house on the island for anyone who wants to take a retreat and I worked there for nearly two years. It was an incredibly good preparation because I had the community life. We were a team of eight and we shared meals together, we lived and worked together and we even shared our prayer together. In the local church there were three services a day – morning and evening prayer and a Communion service.

While I was on Holy Island I got to know the saints. I knew nothing at all about the saints and I'd never thought of them until I went there. I learnt about Celtic Christianity and St Aidan and St Cuthbert. I got to know them and I started to pray to them as they do in the Roman Catholic tradition, and they became real for me. The whole idea of the communion of saints is very important to me. I think there is a link between us and those that have gone before us. They don't have to have been great saints.

The community here still hadn't given me a date when I could join them. I was twiddling my thumbs anxiously. And I used to visit them twice a year so they knew I was still serious about joining them. To fill in time I went to Iona, the island in Scotland where they have another large Christian community. While I was working on Iona, All Saints eventually said I could join them. It was four years after the breakdown.

This community was founded in 1851. In the nineteenth century there was a revival of religious life in both the Roman Catholic and Anglican traditions. Ours was one of the very first communities to be formed after this gap of about three hundred years.

There is a strong movement among religious communities today to rediscover the vision of their founders. Our founder was a well-to-do woman living in London. She decided to live with a few others worshipping God in a regular rhythm of prayer and serving the poor in the slum dwellings around her. It was a pretty pioneering thing to do in those days, when options for women were marriage or be a governess. She and her companions went begging for scraps from hotels and the houses of the rich including those that they had formerly dined with. They must have been looked at rather askance by high society.

At the London House we still do inner-city work with the poor. One of the sisters was recently working on a project in Camden for children with HIV and AIDS.

Today we are 'Sisters of the Poor' and 'poor' is a very broad term. It doesn't just mean those who are penniless and homeless like those 'The Porch' ministers to. This is a drop-in café for the homeless which is open twice a day, morning and evening, six days a week. The Porch started up because we had so many people knocking at the door asking if they could have a cup of tea and a sandwich. There was an elderly sister who used to support them, and it just got out of proportion. We knew that something more formal needed to happen. So we opened up an old apple store in the wall of our convent and now it is this café which offers free tea and coffee and sandwiches. We also now have paid staff there as well as volunteers.

Then of course there is Helen House, which you may know about. If you have a sick and dying child that is another form of poverty. In 1982 Helen House was founded as the world's first hospice for children. Sister Frances Dominica got to know a family whose daughter had a brain tumour which was operated on but it left their daughter, Helen, completely helpless. Frances offered to give her parents a break and look after Helen from time to time. This gave her the idea that there must be lots of other parents in this situation because, although there were adult hospices at the time, there were no children's hospices. So, across our grounds in the garden we formed Helen House. It can now house up to eight children at a time, and the family can stay as well.

They have a paid professional staff who run it, with Frances as the director. She is still very much involved in what goes on.

Also on site is St John's residential home, a home for elderly people which began as a hospital for incurables. Another community, a men's community, the Society of St John the Evangelist, invited our sisters to come and nurse in the hospital and now it's become a residential home which is part of the convent building. Two of our sisters are now being cared for there, including our oldest sister, Sister Pauline, who had her one hundred and first birthday yesterday.

And of course we all have individual ministries here as well as the established ministries on campus. So, as you can see, we are a fairly active community. Interestingly though, with the new revival in the religious life, the enclosed orders who are there specifically to pray and don't go out much and don't have 'works' on site like we do, are attracting more new novices than the active communities. Why that is, I don't know, but the Sisters of the Love of God where you've interviewed Judith is enclosed and they have seven new novices at the moment. It's interesting, isn't it? Their life is so disciplined you'd think it would frighten people away and the reverse is true. But I prefer a more active life, it suits me very well here.

My relationship with God has grown enormously since I've been in community. Partly I think because I'm able to spend more time praying than I did before I came. This gives more opportunity for a relationship to develop with God. Every morning I read the Bible before I go and pray and I mull over one of the readings and think about an idea from it or maybe a verse and then perhaps let that lead into my prayer life and it might help. It doesn't always work but it might help speak to me about a situation I'm in or a problem I've got to wrestle with or it might just be something comforting.

But it's not just when I'm praying that I'm aware of God. I see God in all kinds of ways – in other people, in their friendship. And we have an annual retreat of about six days a year which is silent time set apart just to be alone with God. Well, I say silent but I usually have a guided retreat, so each morning I would see someone, say for forty minutes, who would guide me through the day. And apart from that it's silent for six days or eight days. When you do that annually it can be quite an important moment in your year, because you are reviewing the year that has gone and trying to discover something about yourself and about God in those days, and inevitably something will surface – you might see a relationship in a totally new way or discover that you are nursing a resentment against someone or you might discover that you've had a mental block about something. God might be putting a pointer in a certain direction and you only see it clearly when you take time.

Here we also experience God as a dying child, as we pray all the time for the children at Helen House. The parents of the children often come and use our chapel and talk to the sisters. And I work once a week at The Porch. There can be up to sixteen homeless people there at any one time and there are a lot of problems, drug-related, alcohol-related and of course, mental illness. The people who come find it very valuable as a place where they can just sit and relax and not be hounded on the streets. God is in that, in them. And it is humbling, being with people who haven't got a roof over their head, whereas we have and we are supposed to be 'Sisters of the Poor', and we live in a Victorian palace. That can be quite a problem for us, wrestling with that.

I also find God in music. I find a really good classical concert can be a great aid to prayer. I love Bach – he's my favourite – and Mahler and Mozart. I love the slow movement of Mahler's Fifth Symphony. I love the pathos and the passion, but it's not sentimental. Some would say the music is sentimental because it's become popularised – but I don't think it is, I think it's real music. And Tchaikovsky's *Pathétique*, and Bach's 'Brandenburg' Concertos. Music is available to anyone as a lead in to prayer.

Knowing ourselves and coming to terms with ourselves is one of the most important things in life. That's why the popular idea that if you become a nun or a monk you are running away from life is such a sad misconception. Because the one thing that you can't do wherever you are and whatever you are doing is run away from yourself. In many ways the thing that society offers is a means to run away from yourself like drugs, drink, sex, power, money . . .

When you come into community you are confronted with yourself and certain aspects of yourself that you have not addressed before. It's partly in the nature of living with the same people. Those people get to know you very well and you get to know them extremely well and all the negative stuff can bubble up to the surface. With all the frictions between people. You have to engage with these ongoing relationships. You can't say 'Well, goodbye, I'm going home now.' So relating to the same people day in and day out is part of discovering yourself. What makes you mad about some people and what makes you glad about some people and why.

One of my favourite parts of the day is the silence between the last service of the day and bed when you are by yourself and you are free to reflect on the day that has happened and perhaps to learn something from it, and to pray. You are facing yourself, in relation to these other people and, in that, finding God. You can't find God cut off from other people. God is found amongst other people and in your relationships with them. And that is true for everyone whoever they live with.

Poverty, Chastity and Obedience

Poverty. Well, we take these three vows and the first one is called 'poverty'. But where is poverty in our lifestyle with meals provided and a roof over our heads? So I suppose it is poverty of a certain form. We endeavour to live a life of simplicity. We don't have any luxuries but we are not called to be threadbare. Our monthly allowance covers toothpaste, soap and necessities. And we have a clothing allowance of

£150 a year. But we don't have our own bank accounts or anything and it's difficult to adapt to that.

For me one of the most frustrating aspects of poverty is not the poverty of money but the poverty of time. If you feel like going to see someone you can't just drop everything and go. We do get a free half day a week when we can please ourselves. Of course people who work in a nine-to-five job experience poverty of time as well. Few people are free to do things any time they want, but if I feel like going to see a friend one evening I can't just get up and go. Sometimes I might have a friend who might come here on my half day off and we'll go out for a meal, or even to a concert. I have friends outside who come to visit and we sometimes go out.

The community wears the habit less and less, and although I still wear mine quite a lot because I do a lot of work outside, I don't wear it on my afternoon off or on holiday. But to go back to poverty, we don't pretend we are like the homeless that we work with because that would be patronising. It is somehow trying to align ourselves with the poor of this world by sharing things. Sharing is at the heart of the vow of poverty. We share all our possessions. You can't say 'this is mine' like you can outside.

The thing that was most hard for me to lose was the sea, having lived on Holy Island and Iona before coming here. And I have missed having my own money. Before I joined community I spent quite a lot because I knew it was my last chance. If I liked the look of a blouse or a skirt, I'd go and buy it. But I've adapted.

We are saying 'No' to certain experiences. We can't just go off and do what we like whenever we like. There is a rhythm and a routine which limits us. But in any walk of life you have things that you can't do. If you don't have much money you can't go abroad on holidays. We are all limited. The difference is that we have chosen this life. And it can open up experiences that you might never have had. Before I came into community I had never worked in a drop-in café for the homeless. I'm not saying that is a way-out thing to do but it is just something that I hadn't done before.

* * *

Chastity. Chastity includes celibacy. In the religious life celibacy is a given. You don't have sexual relationships, you forgo that. People think it's awful not to have a partner, but for me the hardest bit of chastity is not so much forgoing sexual relations but the emotional chastity – what goes on in your heart. It is very easy to get too emotionally engaged with other people or with one other person and that can drag on for quite a long time. And if you are in that state of a negative emotional attachment then that can churn you up and it can be draining on your relationship with God.

Chastity is very much to do with the inward state. When you don't make your whole love and commitment to one other human being but God is in this position, then it frees you (this is the ideal I'm talking about) to relate to everyone and to love, in some degree, everyone that you encounter. If you have that one solid-rock relationship with God and you are not tied in any way to one human being you are free to open up to others.

You have more time as well. I find this a lot as guest sister. Often guests just want me to listen to them and they want to pour out their troubles and I find that a great privilege to be in that position as guest sister.

So I said that is the ideal. In reality we are all human beings. Sisters and brothers, monks and nuns have the same emotions that everyone else has. Obviously there is nothing wrong with being emotionally attached to someone, but there it is a question of degree. Just as outside it is all right to be fond of someone who is married to someone else but there is a boundary where too much attachment, even of a purely emotional kind, simply isn't appropriate – it's the same with us. Our primary focus is on God. But you can get very emotionally attached and if there isn't a physical outlet for that, which our life doesn't allow, because we are human, that can be a source of frustration.

That is where prayer becomes so important. Because if you deny what is going on, if you are in that state of being very hooked up to someone and you deny to yourself what is going on, then it can hook you up inside. If you take it honestly to God in prayer and allow God to work on it, it might take a long time, but even with the pain that is involved you can grow through it. You can be drawn closer to God and to others. It's important, as I said, equally for anyone outside who finds themselves thinking about someone that they can't have, for any reason, to recognise it when it is beginning to happen. You're thinking about this person a lot – 'Oh, here we go again.' And just hand it to God and see how God deals with it alongside you. This is not an escape from the emotional life. We still have our emotions which can be very deep and powerful.

And as to our actual sexuality. Well it's still here. It is still part of me and I'm aware of it. It's just that you have to somehow learn to channel it differently. Instead of having an exclusive sexual relationship with one person, whether it's your lover, your boyfriend, your husband or whatever – where you channel all your sexual energy – that energy flows out to others. It doesn't take the form of sexual intercourse, but you can still love people in the quality of the time that you spend with them.

Your sexual energy is still there, rumbling around. You can't deny it. But it is somehow transformed into our love for God. It is not a denial. It's a denial of physical involvement, yes, but it's not a denial of the energy that is behind that. I've not had sexual partners, I've had boyfriends but nothing really serious that lasted, so you could say that I don't know what I'm missing. Maybe it's easier taking a vow of celibacy if you haven't had sexual partners – I'm not sure. Several of the sisters here were very happily married and later widowed. Is celibacy easier for them? I don't know. Lots of people outside are celibate too – either through choice or otherwise. Is it easier for them? Obviously every individual is different. But for me, as I said it is the emotional bit that is the hardest aspect of it. It is for me to get too emotionally attached to someone. It's human nature, isn't it? Join the world, right?

* * *

Obedience. Obedience is traditionally regarded as the hardest of the three vows. And I think it is for me. Of course it's not like the old days where you were blindly obedient. Mother said 'Do this' and you'd do it. There is much more of a consultative relationship. Decisions are made with 'the common mind', which is the community meeting together and making decisions. But having said that, there is a sense in which you are told — or at least strongly suggested — to do things. And I can find it quite a struggle. There are things that are expected of me, practising the organ regularly or whatever — and I just don't do it. I've got a reputation for occasionally not getting to the first service of the day on time — it's at six thirty. Ever since I was at boarding school I've found it hard to get up in the morning. Some days I either totally oversleep and miss the service altogether, or am late. I was late this morning. Sometimes it is just dismissed with a gentle smile and sometimes I'm called to account, especially if I'm just not there. I now have two alarm clocks. I always knew that God was not calling me to be an enclosed sister where they have a service in the middle of the night. I just knew that God does not ask the impossible.

On the plus side of obedience, it is good to have someone else to refer to in making decisions, especially important decisions, or in daily tasks even. Self-deception is the easiest thing in the world and you can easily get a bee in your bonnet and think that 'this is what God is asking me to do'. And if you don't sound it out with someone else first it could be totally wrong and lead you up the creek. So I think it's quite useful to have a mechanism in place where a set of people or one person at least is in authority and you can sound out your ideas with them and they can sound out their ideas with you. You can come to a common mind ideally about what the best plan of action is.

We all also have a spiritual director. You have someone you can go to who is like a spiritual friend and say what is happening and ask what they think. Just by talking it through you realise what you yourself think. So although hierarchy is not a very popular concept these days it can be quite useful to have a structure whereby people check each other out. The Mother checks herself with others, as well. It's not a question of one person dictating.

We are all subject to Christ. That's the pattern. He is the one that we are being obedient to but we are channelling that obedience through those set over us in the community. Like the chastity model where you are channelling your love for God not through one person but through all the people that you encounter. Here you are channelling your obedience to God and Christ through those set over you in community.

If there was something that I particularly wanted to do I'd approach Mother Helen and ask her. She'd either say 'Yes' immediately or she might want to sound it out with some of the other sisters, especially if there was money involved. So far I've never asked to do anything and had anyone say 'No'.

As for being asked to do things that I don't want to do, Mother Helen would like me to learn to use the word processor but I'm not making very good progress on that. I don't feel I have an aptitude for it. Or maybe I've just decided that because I don't want to do it!

Part of the role and call of Religious Life is a prophetic role. By which I mean trying to see the signs of the times and speaking out about things as and when it is necessary. It is good for religions to get together and petition MPs, to strive for justice. Our grace before lunch today was: 'To those who are hungry give food, and to those who have food give a hunger for justice.' That's one of Mother Helen's favourites. And that's where the kingdom of God comes in, in seeking justice for the oppressed and seeking food for the hungry. We need to redress the balance in society and turn things upside down. Historically nuns and monks have always been at the forefront of the fight for justice. Today, well, the work of our community as regards homelessness is The Porch which is only a tiny little bit. If I wanted to go to a demonstration I'm sure they would support me. We have a sister who is very interested in working for justice and peace issues and in July the Lambeth Conference of the Church of England has invited each religious community to send up to three people to a debate on world debt. Many of the communities are supporting Jubilee 2000 – I was reading an article yesterday in the *Anglican Communities Year Book* by a novice, Sister Emma at Tymawr, about Jubilee 2000, the campaign to cancel the unrepayable debts of the poorer countries. She is encouraging us all to write to our MPs, MEPs and the Director of the IMF.

Once I was going to preach in our parish church. I was doing a drama. It was Pentecost, which is the day when we celebrate the gift of the Holy Spirit. The church was full of children; just as we were about to practise this man walked in off the street and walked right up to the altar and said in a loud voice, 'I am Jesus Christ.' He was totally out of it. He just walked out quietly and we got on with the drama and had the service but it really touched me. I felt quite hopeless in that situation. I wasn't frightened or freaked out – I just felt helpless, and the only thing I could do was stand and watch until he walked out. Here we were doing our nice organised drama and we weren't touching on his need at all. OK – it wasn't the right time or place, but where is he now? Who's helping him? We are surrounded by people like that in east Oxford. At the moment a lot of our work is taken up with people who come to the convent. All kinds of people come and stay. If we had more young novices here we'd be freer to think about what further ministries we'd like to engage in. I'd like to be able to do more work in the community.

What don't I like about the life here? Well, the worst thing about life in the community, and I'm certainly not saying that I'm free of this myself, but it's amazing how people can get caught up in details. Tiny things can suddenly become very important like 'Who put the milk where?' or 'What happened to the bread?' or 'You can't eat that!' It's often around food, funnily enough. These petty little outbursts can come along – it drives me crazy. And sometimes we end up in these long meetings. They certainly have the ability sometimes to become heavy and long-winded and bogged down and I just long to walk out the door and get some fresh air. Those kind of things I find really difficult.

Things are changing all the time here. When I first visited this community people wore habits all the time with a veil. Then there was an experiment to alter the habit, so in the end I didn't have any choice, I had to get rid of the veil and adopt this new-style habit which is all in one piece. I've got used to no veil and I like it; it can be quite restricting. I feel a greater freedom not having a veil and it's all tied in historically with male dominance and the idea in the Bible in St Paul that a woman has to cover her head to worship. So there is a sense of freedom from that, in a funny kind of way.

We have discussions about the habit. Should we stop wearing a habit? Now we have set times when we have to wear it such as Sundays, big feast days and public occasions. But otherwise for normal days it doesn't have to be worn. You'll have noticed that several sisters today were in mufti. I wear the habit more than most of them because for me it is tied up with my sense of vocation. I told you about when I was reading Isaiah and I had this strong sense of me being a nun and being in a habit and so, for me, it is very bound up with my sense of call and it is quite important for me to wear it.

Sometimes people can feel cheated if you are not wearing a habit and they get to know you and divulge things to you, and then they find out you are a sister and they think, 'Oh gosh, I wish that I hadn't said that.' It can work both ways.

So here I am, in my new habit, and I'd like to stay and take life vows if the sisters will have me. Sometimes it still seems a little strange, the idea of becoming a nun, even though I am one. My family were taken aback to begin with about me being here. My mother would naturally have liked me to have got married and have had children but now she's got used to the idea, and if I told her that I wasn't going to take life vows she'd be quite upset. She's got to know the sisters and likes them and sees that I'm happy in the life. So watch this space, we'll have to see whether the sisters will accept me for life.

At the time of going to press Margaret Anne is on holiday on her beloved Iona. The Sisters have accepted her for life and she hopes to take her life vows this year. 'I feel I belong here now,' she grins widely.

sister joan

*I had never been to church in my life and when I did go, I
was astounded to find that, after the service, people
discussed the social events and the local news. I wanted to
talk about the reality of God in our lives at a deep level.
It never crossed my mind to approach the Vicar.*

sister joan

SOCIETY OF THE SACRED CROSS

GWENT, WALES

I travelled to find the Society of the Sacred Cross by public transport, an exercise that I would not recommend, as the convent is remote, to say the least. Tucked snugly into idyllic countryside in the Wye Valley, the community has the instant effect of making you want to stay for ever. Furthermore, they grow almost all their own food, and the lunch I was given there (everything home-made including the bread) was unforgettable.

The Mother in this community (who does not call herself 'Mother' but 'Sister') has another of those passing smiles which, despite a thirty-second meeting, made a very definite impression on me, like being bathed in kindness.

Sister Joan, is forty-one years old, and one of two novices in the tiny enclosed community of only fifteen sisters. As we sat with the window open, the sound of bird song was recorded along with the gentle voice of Sister Joan. She spoke with great humility as if surprised that anyone should take interest in her imminent decision to live the rest of her life in a remote convent.

This community differs from others in that we work out our own programme around the services. There are no fixed times for reading or work. I get up at 5.30 every morning and begin each day with one hour of silent prayer. If you persevere over a period of time, your body easily gets used to getting up early. After the first service, which is at seven, there is breakfast. Then I might do some chores or go out into the kitchen garden and dig up some vegetables for lunch. We grow most of our own fruit and vegetables here – it's wonderful. The next service is at 8.45; then we may have a meeting and then I'm supposed to have study time. I say 'supposed to' because although I enjoy the study, I often end up doing more chores – but I'm trying to be more disciplined about the study. The Communion service is at 12.00 and then after lunch we have half an hour of rest in our rooms. I sometimes sleep, or doze at any rate. From 2 to 2.45 I may read some kind of spiritual book and then I work again until about 5.15. Then chapel again, evening prayer, supper, work until 7 when I have half an hour's free time. At 7.30 I go back to chapel for an hour's silent prayer before the night service at 8.30. After night prayer, I'm up to my room by 9.00 and the light is usually out by 9.30.

I am the eldest in my family. I have one brother who is almost five years younger than I am. My parents never went to church and my only experience of church as a child was the once-a-week service that we all had to go to at the local C of E junior school. We never went to Sunday school. We just weren't a church-going family at all. We didn't even go at Christmas. I went to the local mixed secondary modern school, having managed to fail my eleven plus and not get into the local high school.

I hated school. I remember my dad saying, 'School days are the happiest days of your life' and I used to think, 'Heaven help me if these really are the happiest days.' I think I was miserable because I was only a very average student and I was utterly hopeless at maths. I was a bit of a loner and was always happiest by myself. I wasn't a party person from my earliest childhood and the difficulties I had at school I didn't want to share with anyone. Not with friends or family. I think at sixteen or seventeen I was quite immature and painfully shy. I was far too timid to go hunting for boys and if one had come along they would soon have got fed up because I was so withdrawn. I ended up with about two O levels and about nine CSEs which were absolutely useless. I did further education and ended up with five O levels and a secretarial qualification. The careers office sent me to the civil service and I got a job with the Department of Employment in Birmingham.

I think through this time I was searching for something. I had hundreds of fads. I would cotton on to one idea, like archaeology, and turn up as a volunteer on a dig with my little brush and teaspoon. Then that would wear off. I had a spell of gardening and took over the garden at home, turning everything upside down. I was going to plant all these wonderful things and I think I did for about one season and that was it. I'd done that. I remember sewing, dress-making and hiking, and then at one stage I had a go at learning Gaelic. I was going to go around the remote islands of Scotland speaking to the local people in fluent Gaelic!

Meanwhile, I took more exams in the civil service in order to move up and get promoted. Every so many years I was recommended to be moved up to a new post and I finally ended up as the supervisor in the finance section, which, despite my lack of maths, I enjoyed very much. I worked for Redditch Skillcentre and then in Worcester on the Youth Training Scheme. I enjoyed it all very much.

I had bought my own house by this time and found, in a way that is difficult to explain, I was feeling drawn to God. It was odd never having been to church in my life and not having any family or friends that went to church. Once or twice I sneaked into a service and went in secret. And I remember a TV programme about a monastery. I was so moved by the words of some of the monks who were seeking God in such a single-minded way. I knew it touched something in me – as if I knew that this is what true life is all about, to seek God. Seeking God is the purpose of life. And I watched these monks and thought that this is the life I would love. I was about twenty-seven at that time and still outside the Church.

When I was twenty-nine, I saw a poster advertising Billy Graham's 'Mission England'. It was at the Aston Villa football ground and I knew I wanted to go but I didn't want to get involved with all these strange 'Christians'; they were far too weird. It was all very embarrassing. But the reason I went was to make some public declaration of faith. It wouldn't have mattered what Billy Graham had said because I had decided beforehand I wanted to go forward. I remember praying that this wouldn't be just another passing fad.

I then started to go to church. There was a wide range of services – to cater for everyone – from the 1662 Prayer Book service to the very evangelical praise and worship services with guitars and noise. I joined the church choir and so I was involved in the whole lot and I found I was increasingly drawn to the quiet ones. But there was a deep spiritual part of me that the local church wasn't meeting.

So from the ages of twenty-nine to thirty-four this 'spiritual longing' came and went and I very much felt it had to be all or nothing. Then it would go away. But over the period the times when I felt I wanted to pursue God in a wholehearted way got greater and greater, and in some corner of my mind I remembered this TV documentary. I had never been to a monastery or a convent in my life, but I reached a stage where I felt an increasing dissatisfaction with my life.

I went to the local library and read up on Anglican communities, feeling particularly drawn to the contemplative rather than the active ones. From a list of about twenty I eventually went to visit the Community of St Clare in Freeland, Oxford. I was totally in fear of these 'holy' people and the thought that I had ever considered joining them seemed quite absurd. They seemed totally out of my league.

They seemed like 'special spiritual people that were so close to God'. Surely I could never aspire to anything like that? So I spent four lovely days at Freeland and didn't do anything more about it for about two years.

I think I was called and that I am being called. What I have come to believe, from my understanding at this point in time, is that in every single person is something deep within us, at the root of us. That is part of God. That is God. And that God who created us loves us so much that he calls us, draws us, but it is in the deepest part of us. This root of us is searching, it wants fulfilment, it wants completeness, it wants God, basically. Because God has put that within us, he is calling each of us to himself. Because it is only by coming to God, through meeting with God, that we will find our true joy, true life, and will find that true fulfilment. I believe he has put that in every single person and all these searchings, all this going after other 'things' and people, looking for this completeness and a truly fulfilled life – well, none of those things can actually satisfy at all. They may do for a short time but the truth is that we will only feel any true satisfaction if we can allow ourselves to be drawn to him. Then we can 'know'. It is there all the time, but we can know joy and peace and fulfilment.

Even at the very early stages that I'm at, I feel as if I've had little 'tastes' and that I am at the beginning of something, but it is enough for me to know that God is the only source of true contentment and true peace. It is a real happiness, a real joy, and it is only because of God drawing us to himself. So, looking back, I do feel that God has been calling me from when I was a little child. I can see it in those lonely and difficult times when I felt burdened with so many cares at such a young age, and I do believe that Christ was there all the way through that. It just took me a long time to recognise that it was God calling me. I think the calling will go on through the rest of my life. It seems very complicated. For me it is very simple but I find it hard to put into words.

In my heart I have a deep longing that is sometimes more intense than at others. Not just when I'm in prayer but at other times too. Sometimes there is a clarity when I understand and see the love of God, the love of God for me, his/her gentleness, tenderness, care and humility. But it isn't just thoughts 'about' God; it is actually almost . . . well, not touching those things of God, but there is a clarity that God is there in that gentle way. Sometimes the experience – experiencing something of that gentleness and tenderness and beauty – brings a response in my heart of such longing to give myself to God. There is something about seeing the beauty of God . . . sometimes the feeling is so intense that I feel my heart is going to burst out of my chest. I feel I want to physically take my heart and give it to God. That is in response to an 'awareness' of the gentleness of God, his respect almost, his love.

Sometimes, particularly in times of prayer, occasionally if things have been difficult, I have come to God and felt totally enveloped in peace . . . and felt such relief . . . and sighed 'Thank you Lord.' But that doesn't happen very often and a lot of the time, in truth, in coming to prayer there are no feelings. Sometimes I can have an hour's silent prayer and feel that nothing has happened in that hour. Sometimes my mind is racing over all sorts of different thoughts and I find it very hard to still my mind. Even if I am physically still, I sometimes find it hard to still my mind. So in that state it is harder to experience God.

I find that more recently I can say to God in a surer way, in a real way, 'Lord, I trust you with my life.' And I feel that I can, and that it is safe because of the love of God. It is almost like knowing that God is there as a loving God. So, even when there aren't those intense times, there is a growing and it is still very small really, but there is a growing sense of God's presence. Is this all a bit vague?

Sometimes I am given insights – or maybe that is too grand a way of putting it! Sometimes I will see something quite new in a passage of Scripture. For example, in the last eighteen months or so, it has been like an insight into the relationship Christ had with God. Like in the time when he was in the garden of Gethsemane, and at his trial, it is almost like entering into it, and yet not entering in. This is hard. Well having an understanding, seeing clearly for an instant the relationship, the total trust . . . the trust and the love that was so 100 per cent that Christ allowed himself to rest in God's hands, to be handed over. He was utterly defenceless, totally dependent on God. There is so much more to it than that. So any growth that I have towards God has been in understanding the depth and intimacy of that relationship and feeling that I want to be drawn into that and be able to have that sort of a relationship with God.

When I came here, I think I thought that the response was mine and that I was coming to God as an independent person. I was coming to God. What I've now understood more is that I can't come to God of myself; I am only responding to God and it is God who is drawing me. When I came, I felt I wanted to give myself to God. There was a desperation. There is still a certain amount of desperation and longing for God but I felt it was all coming from me and I wanted God to accept me. The growth has come, in that it has turned around, and I now see that it is God drawing me and that it is all intertwined. This shift has taken place over the last two years through Scripture and through prayer.

Your reader may be thinking, 'This is all very well, but I don't find God answers my prayers.' My own experience is of a God who loves so much, who wants to give himself/herself so much. But that doesn't help the reader much. Maybe it depends on our understanding of prayer? Do I understand what prayer is? Well, for me, it is to come before God and to try to be open for God to come to me. Or maybe it is more of that two-way thing? I am coming to God in prayer, seeking God, and trying to be open to receive. When I pray I don't feel I am an intercessor. Here we pray for the world and for all parts of the world and for people who have asked for our prayers. But I don't quite know how God uses our prayer . . . I believe that God may use each of us for special intercession from time to time, but that what God primarily wants is to come into our lives.

When there is suffering, I know that God can work through suffering. I don't think he causes suffering but I think he can work through it. The world that we live in, our own human nature, all sorts of things may be a cause of suffering and I believe God can work through it. I have experienced painful times myself and it is hard at the time when you are going through pain and it hurts you, but . . . perhaps this is more what I'm longing for more than what actually is . . . I hope that, instead of looking for comfort in other things, it will bring me running to God. This is beginning to sound like a theory and I don't want it to be like that.

Some of the sisters here could say that they have talked to people who have come here seeking help, who have been suffering a lot and who have come through it with a much stronger faith – but quite how or why I don't really know. . . I don't have an answer.

Poverty, Chastity and Obedience

Poverty. Well, what always comes to mind for most people is, 'What are you giving up?' And the answer in my case is my job with my great salary and my pension and my good holidays . . . and I have given up my bungalow, which I loved. At the moment I still have my car here but it won't be mine much longer. For me it was difficult coming to the decision to resign the job and sell my bungalow but my 'all or nothing for God' made me feel that, in comparison with what I was gaining, these were very little and they weren't so hard to give up. Call it a romantic ideal if you like, but I felt that I wanted to come to be where I feel totally stripped of everything so that I am all there for God. I am all God's. So in some ways it wasn't too painful. The joy! Maybe it will sound false but it's true . . . the joy underlies everything. I mean there are days when it gets quite tough here and I sometimes end up in tears because I feel it is so awful. But on the whole, I have discovered a joy and a satisfaction in being drawn to God, that has become like the treasure that they speak about in Scripture. It's that 'giving-up-everything-for-that-one-pearl' type thing!

I have found something that is so much greater and so much more fulfilling than anything I have given up, and I feel that this is what my life is all about. It is the life within. It is the knowing God that makes the letting go of all the other stuff comparatively easy.

★ ★ ★

Chastity. Well there were three men in my life who would have liked a serious relationship but I did not want that myself. So from the start, I gave them no encouragement. I went out with them but I never wanted to be married, so as soon as they started to get serious I ended it. These men were OK as friends but I didn't really love any of them enough. One actually suggested marriage, but I wasn't interested. So, no, I never had sexual relations with any of them. I've never seen myself in the role of 'wife' or 'mother', either, for that matter. I don't know why. My brother is married and he has two boys and they are lovely but I love them as my nephews. I have never wanted to be in either of those roles.

Intimacy for me has been reserved for God. Having not experienced sex myself, maybe I don't know what I'm giving up, but what I have experienced here is so wonderful. I can only imagine that it is like the feeling you would get in an intimate relationship with another human being when it is all going well. I feel it more than compensates for what I have given up. I don't dwell too much on what I'm missing. Maybe I'm strange. My focus is on God. With all the vows, they are all the same, really. They are different aspects of the same desire which is saying, 'Only you Lord.'

★ ★ ★

Obedience. Well again the view outside community seems to be that this consists in being asked to do something, and that you have to obey regardless of whether it seems good or bad or right or wrong. To me it means not responding out of duty but rather out of love. Again like the relationship between Christ and God. Jesus suffered all that he suffered, and that sort of obedience is obedience of love.

What I'm hoping for is to be able to respond to things in a Christ-like way. What happens in reality is that, when I'm asked to go and work in the kitchen, I feel 'I'd really rather not and I really don't want to do that', but I do it anyway. I'm hoping eventually that I will be able to do things more graciously. They are thoughts and not words and I do what I'm asked to do, but they are still thoughts.

It sounds a bit dramatic to say that one of the reasons that I wanted to live the Religious Life was to learn to 'die to myself'. All the things that get in the way between me and God, I want them to go. I see all the vows as different aspects of ways to transform myself into being more God-centred. They are all different facets of the same attitude.

On a more practical level, of course, there are things here that drive me crazy. I don't like the sung Communion service on Sundays because none of us sing very well and, with apologies to Sister Anne, our choir mistress, I would much rather have a spoken service. I prefer silent meals to talking ones. I don't like it when we have to socialise and chatter to each other over food. I find the turnover of guests here quite exhausting – too many guests too quickly, and I find it very difficult. But these are only little things.

My mum now goes to church. I don't think my dad really understands what I'm doing. He was worried when I gave up my good job and my bungalow. My friends and working companions were very supportive. My manager held my job open for ten months, and I still hadn't made up my mind, so they extended it for another four months. When I eventually resigned, they sent me a wonderful letter offering me my job back if I felt I had made the wrong decision.

Occasionally, if I'm in a stubborn mood, I'll think, 'I'm not going down to chapel to pray', but I've never missed a service. As novices we don't have spending money in this community but I had some money and I remember buying chocolate. This is about the greatest rebellion

I've made so far, spending some of my own money on chocolate!

I want more and more joy for the sisters here and for it to show in our services, our praise and our worship. Sometimes I feel sad because we just seem to say the Office without really thinking about what we are saying or who we are saying it to.

Maybe you can't have that all the time. One of the sisters said that, when you have been married for about fifty years, the relationship changes and deepens and becomes more mellow. Sister Jeanne is ninety-three and has been here for sixty years, so her relationship with God is understandably rather different from mine. But sometimes, when we have meetings, I just have to say something about how wonderful God is and make a right fool of myself.

Shortly after this interview Sister Joan was accepted for a further three years and another new novice has joined the Gwent community.

As a part of their hospitality, the Tymawr sisters welcome both men and women to work and pray with them for up to three months.

sister rose

*I went to this church for the first time in my life and there
was all this fussing about going on up at the front and
I said 'What's all this?' And the priest said it was the
Last Supper and where to read it in the Bible and
stuff and I read it. 'Do this in remembrance of me.'
Jesus was sitting at a meal table, and there they are
swinging incense over the holy book and all. And I
thought, and I still think it now, 'How did they get
from that to this performance?'*

sister rose

Visiting Rose in Brixton was more like calling in to a friend's house for lengthy chats than conducting interviews in a convent. The semi-detached suburban house is just like any other home, only one room is a chapel — a very beautiful and simple chapel with cream walls, green carpet and a figure of a black Christ crucified.

Rose joined the Franciscan order three years ago. She does have a habit but wears it only for rare formal occasions. When I met her she wore a brightly coloured patchwork skirt she had made herself. Salad was prepared in the kitchen. We sat and ate before resorting to the sofas and the floor in the lounge. I met none of the other sisters who were out at work, but the house has an atmosphere of gentleness.

I didn't really interview Rose at all. I asked her one question and then she just talked while I sat back and relaxed. She is such a gifted speaker, although she does not consider herself as such, I asked

*if she had ever considered becoming a priest. I visualised her leading
a church community in the East End with her self-deprecating
humour and joy. She said 'I'd rather be dead than be a parish
priest.' I hope she changes her mind some day soon.*

*Every word of her interview was first-class entertainment. Editing
it was agony as I didn't want to lose a single sentence. Rose
merits a book to herself.*

I come from Dagenham. It's mostly people live there who like my
parents were born in the East End. That's why I talk like this. People
from Dagenham sound Cockney and talk like I do. I know all the
grammar's wrong but that's the way I talk. I tell you who else comes
from Dagenham: the Archbishop of Canterbury and Dudley Moore
and me. He's a self-made man, the Archbishop of Canterbury, because
they don't talk like him in Dagenham. He's got a doctorate as well,
and they don't get doctorates in Dagenham, neither. He left school at
fourteen.

I come from this council estate, the largest council estate in Europe.
I've got two sisters, one older and one younger. No religious
upbringing at all. Well, we were christened, but my family didn't know
it was anything religious. They had no thought for things like that. I
had godparents but they didn't believe in God. When I asked my nan
about it once – where the other nan had gone when she died – I
thought maybe she'd gone somewhere, I suspected she didn't just go
in the ground. I was fourteen, and she said to me, 'Look you get born,
you live, you die and you go in there, that's it.' And I knew she was
wrong. That made a mockery of this life. Anyway she was my
godmother.

We went to Sunday school a couple of times, and you could win a
rubber or a pencil with a text on it if you answered a question right,
but I never won anything. I went to church a bit with the Brownies
and Guides. But you had to. God wouldn't have been a topic that

would ever have been discussed. You didn't discuss things in Dagenham in the fifties, you watched telly. You didn't think things. If you thought things, you soon learned that wasn't normal for there, so then you just thought them in your head. People said, 'What do you want to worry about that for?' or 'Don't worry yourself about it.'

We had a really tiny house. I went back to Dagenham with Joyce, the Australian Novice Guardian, and she said 'How did five people live in that house?' It was really tiny. We walked round the corner to the school and I remembered I only ever liked one teacher, but there was a dinner lady with blue nylon overalls called Mrs McKenzie and Joyce said, 'What do you think her first name was?' and I said, 'It was probably Lou' and Joyce stood on the pavement and said right out loud, 'I salute you, Lou McKenzie!' She's going like that and I thought 'Fancy coming back here all these years later to pay tribute to this woman.' She was very important to me, this dinner lady. She's like something there in your life that gave you a bit of meaning at the school. I remember the rustle of the nylon overall. She was a solid grandmotherly type she was.

My father was a policeman. He joined the police because a police house come with the job. We were living at my nan's at the time, the four of us in one bedroom. People in Dagenham at that time worked at Ford or at the docks, but my dad was a copper. My mum was a machinist. She went into that at fourteen. They didn't think about education. There was a lot of people missed out.

When I was nine we moved to Ilford and I went to school there. There was forty-eight in the class. I can still count the kids from off the school photo. I didn't find any problem adjusting. I always had friends. Me and my sisters, we always had friends, but it wasn't a very nice school. Then the one I left wasn't very nice either. You sat in rows again, and I was in the stream where they primed you up to do the eleven plus. I had a lot of friends and a laugh and stuff but I was a nonentity. I passed the eleven plus and I was the first one out of our family, cousins as well, to go to the grammar school, and my Mum said, 'Oh God – I thought you could have gone to Mayfield and had your sister's uniform.' My sister said 'You're so poncy dressed up in that.' She told everyone I scraped through. I wasn't borderline but she told her friends I was. So I had to be bought this posh uniform.

There was a lower school and an upper school and I loved the lower school, but, when we left to go to the upper school, I went into a depression that lasted five years. I didn't work very much but I liked doing English and maths. I could write well. I don't write like how I speak. I can write really posh. That's what everyone did in Dagenham. You knew you didn't write 'ain't', but you wouldn't have said 'isn't' because everyone would have laughed you off the face of the earth.

Anyway I was mouthy, lippy as a teenager. If you could get sent out of the lesson you could hop off to the toilet and have a cigarette. I loved sitting in front of the bedroom mirror with lipstick on and smoke and see if I looked sixteen. I was thirteen. I thought people might speak to you directly when you were sixteen. They'd speak to your parents, you know, like 'Does he take sugar?' Although I laughed all the time, I was depressed underneath.

My nan died. I didn't like her. That woman didn't even like her dog. After they lowered the coffin into the ground, I asked my RE teacher if anything happened after you died and he said he didn't know. I really wanted to talk about God but the people at the Christian fellowship at school were swots, the sort of people who were made into head girls and prefects. There was no way I could ask any of them. Yet I suspected something. I thought about things and they didn't. I'd have been all right if I hadn't come from Dagenham.

I never had any self-esteem. I look back now and I think that in order to have self-esteem, you have to be given it all the time you're growing up. And people didn't do that. My parents didn't have any self-esteem. My mother doesn't have any confidence at all. She'd say it's because she doesn't speak nice. And I'll say, 'Other people who don't speak nice have got confidence, so what's the real reason?' She thinks that's the real reason.

For me, I know you have to be taught that you're OK and I never felt that. I'd say now I had a poor self-image and a sense of worthlessness. I didn't have words for it then but I can easily put words to it now. But kids know things they don't have words for.

Once I was in trouble again, and I was sent to the headmistress. She said, 'You're only like this because you are so insecure.' I lay down on the carpet, which was unusual behaviour in the headmistress' office in the sixties. I wanted to faint, but I couldn't pretend to faint because I knew my face wouldn't go white. And I said, 'I don't want to go on any more.' I used to take about twelve aspirins a day twice a week so that I could feel ill. I suppose I thought someone might notice that I wasn't OK. I was quite depressed. She took me to the doctor who sent me to the mental hospital to see a psychiatrist. I was sixteen.

We sat in there – my father had to come – and he said to my father, 'Why is she crying?' He didn't ask me. And my father said, 'I dunno' – it was probably because I was in a mental hospital. He said, 'Next week I'll see you with your mother and then the following week with both of them.' I thought the week after that he might ask to see me alone. But he never did. This was Goodmayes Hospital in Essex in 1969. They wanted to admit me but I wouldn't let them, I had my school work to do. I was just very depressed but I was so inarticulate about it, which I suppose was normal for my age.

Anyway I got four O levels, which was a miracle considering the circumstance, and I left school. No one in Dagenham ever stayed on. I went to start nursing but I was in a terrible state. I was very loud but I had no confidence. When I was eighteen, I started my nurse training. I remember getting pins and needles in my head and the doctor prescribed tranquillisers. They totally disconnected me from myself and I got worse, and eventually they sent me to a mental hospital and admitted me for a year.

Since I've been in community, I've managed to get my notes from that hospital. They had diagnosed me with 'inadequate personality', which is a bit of a bloody cheek as I was only eighteen. Anyway, a year later I was still loud and depressed and they sent me to an aftercare hostel. The bloke who ran it said to me, 'You've never been mentally ill. You've just had a traumatic adolescence.' He was an amazing bloke, a Christian, and he talked to me. In the hospital they never talked to you, they just pilled you up.

I said to this bloke, 'I'm quite interested in your God and stuff, but I don't know how to get it. I can't read the Bible because I know I'm going to hit the virgin birth; if I can't believe that, I can't believe the rest of it.' So he said, 'Just skip the virgin birth and just go straight into Christ beginning his ministry. You're always talking to me and telling me you like people with integrity. You see if you think this bloke's got integrity.' So I said 'OK' and I goes off reading it, and I think that this bloke's absolutely fantastic. And I went back to him and I said, 'This bloke's dynamic.' And he's going to me, 'But do you think he's got integrity?' I loved that word, 'cos I'd just learnt it and I said, 'Yes. But don't push it.' And he didn't.

By this time I was working as an occupational therapist with long-stay patients in a psychiatric ward. I ran a Christmas cracker factory in a psychiatric hospital. One of the nurses told me that she thought I should visit this convent. I wrote to them and asked if I could bring a friend and could they please not mention God. And they wrote and said 'yes', and so I went. I remember they had a crucifix in every room, even in the toilet. You couldn't even do a wee in peace, and the first thing I did was take down the crucifix in my room so I could get undressed. Anyway, I went to the chapel and I could feel the prayer. I didn't know what it was but I could feel it. The last night I was there they had a quarter of an hour silence in the dark with just the sanctum light on, and I was sitting there and I got converted. It was like an injection through me and it completely turned my world upside down. It was wonderful and it was awful and I knew that was God. I asked them what they were and they said they was Anglican and I didn't know what that was and they said it was Church of England, and I thought I must be meant to be one of them. If they'd been Catholic or Baptist, I'd have been one of them. Anyway, I goes back to my friend and I says, 'You won't believe what's happened to me.'

Anyway, I found a vicar and got confirmed, and then two years later I joined the convent. They had made me wait two years; I was twenty-two when I joined them. It was one of them communities with all the black gear. I spent three and a half years there. I did the full novitiate and then I left. The sisters said that I needed to live a bit of life more. They was happy to have me back after two or three years but they wanted me to go out and work and get some therapy. They didn't think I was ready to stay and I knew I wasn't.

The next couple of years I did lots of different jobs. I worked with this one girl in an office and she said to me, 'Exactly how many skirts have you got?' and I said, 'Three.' And she said, 'I'd rather be dead than have three skirts', and I said, 'Well, I'd rather be dead than be a person who'd rather be dead than have three skirts.' I thought that was the saddest person I'd ever met, but I come to like her. I did other odd jobs. I still wanted to join the convent, but I wasn't really emotionally stable enough. You have to be ever so stable in these places where you are silent most of the time. You've no idea how stable you've got to be to survive. Well, either that or you've got to be able to sit on yourself. That is, one of the sisters in this convent said, 'We can't always wear our hearts on our sleeves.' And, when I told one of the sisters here that years later, she said, 'Why didn't you say "Why not?" '

Anyway, I moved to Somerset with a friend and I'd met a couple of blokes by this time, and that had . . . er, altered me in many ways! I won't say no more. Anyway, I was working in Marks and Spencer and I met this girl who was doing an A level and she happened to have written an essay on a book I'd just read, and I told her I'd like to read her essay and, well, to cut a long story short, I ended up doing the class and getting my A level. The teacher told me I could do a degree and I thought the teacher was kidding me and I said, 'Was you serious?' And she was and I did my degree and I got a 2/1. Everyone was pretending to be so naffed off when we got the certificates, but I was so pleased with myself. I even put my glasses on to have my photo taken. And then I did my teacher training and went into teaching and suddenly I had the money for a house and a car and magazines and a take-away if I didn't want to cook.

Anyway, in the first year at college, we did hedonism; and I'd decided to become a hedonist after I'd found out that it meant a pleasure-seeker and I thought, 'I could do with some of that.' I'd tried to be religious all these years and nothing worked out so I thought, 'I'll be a hedonist.' I stopped going to church and praying, and for three years on Sunday morning I'd go to the video shop and get three tapes for six quid and watch them one after the other and I'd read the tabloid Sunday papers. That's being a hedonist. It was doing whatever I wanted. It was pathetic really. It was utterly boring. There is no challenge.

Anyway, one day it was Good Friday and it was one o'clock and God came for me − when I couldn't even be bothered to speak to him. I sort of prayed in a very reluctant way and I felt the Holy Spirit, really strong like I had the first time, and I sat in the bath and cried and I knew I wanted to join the Franciscans and I knew this was it. I knew I'd been on a path to nowhere.

I wanted to finish the school year to see my kids through, the ones I was teaching, and so I had to wait eighteen months. The head offered me my job back if it didn't work out, and I learnt all about the Franciscans. We are dead different from the others. We are more like the Roman Catholics, who are much more liberated now than the Anglican communities. It was far more right for me and eighteen months later I joined. I was forty.

This community started off in the East End in 1905. They took in washing and looked after people's kids to survive, and later ran a nursing home while they lived in a house that was condemned. Then they moved to Somerset and still ran a nursing home for some years. We've got brothers. They started after us. There are a lot more of them than there are of us. When you start as a novice, you have some training with the novice brothers. At the moment there are five women in the novitiate and ten novice friars. We meet up for classes so you get to know them quite well. There's an intake every September. There are forty-one women in the community and about a hundred and twenty men.

The work varies. The largest house in Somerset takes in guests for retreat and spiritual guidance. In this house, one of us is a hospital chaplain, one has just done a massage course, one works in religious vocational guidance, one works in a hospice and I work in Clapham with homeless people who are getting off alcohol. Three of us are on part-time wages but all the money goes into a central fund so that some people can do voluntary work. At Newcastle-under-Lyme where I'm going next, they have guests for quiet days, but I'll be working outside the community as well for some days each week because I want to continue working with the homeless. As a novice in this community, you do a year at Somerset, one year in Brixton and one in Newcastle. But they let me stay here for two years. Because I'm so happy, and I needed to stay, they extended it for me. After that you settle somewhere for longer. Each house is quite different and they want you to see as many ways of living in community and to have lived with as many different sisters as possible before you come up for vows.

We have half an hour's private prayer and then say the morning prayers together from 7.30 till 8; then we have breakfast and go off to work. In the evening you have another half-hour prayer time on your own and then we say the evening prayers at 6 and we take turns to cook supper. We eat at 7.30 and then we say compline at 8.30 and you do what you like after that. Once a week we have a priest who comes in to give a Communion service, and we try and have as many women priests as we can. We have a rota and we have four women out of seven. We are very supportive of women in the Church. We have four sisters who are priests and a couple who are exploring the idea. I find that really good.

One of the things I love about this community is the way you can find out what's right for you in terms of ministry. Like, when I came here, I had no idea I was going to work with the homeless. I was frightened of homeless people, I'd walk past them quick, and then I found that was what I wanted to do. I met this Roman Catholic novice and she was telling me about this soup kitchen where she worked and I thought I could do that. It was at this place where they was de-toxing and getting off the drink and I thought I'd like to work there. I prayed about it for two days and it felt right so I told the novice guardian that was where I'd like to go and she said to 'go up and see them'. I'd only been in there two minutes and I knew. It had a shabby wonderful homely holiness about it. It's run by three Catholic Fathers, not in habits or anything, and one bloke who is celibate but he's not in an order or anything. He's just under his own personal vows to the priest. And there is all different people there and it's very emotionally hyped-up. People have a lot of anger when they are getting off the drink but it's one of the most wonderfully hopeful places I've been to.

People have asked me how I pray. That's a bit like asking how do you think. I experience God as a God of compassion. I'm getting into the feminine in God as well. Because we are brought up with God as he, so I try to use 'she' in my mind when I'm praying on my own. And in some of our services we do try as well to redress the balance. God to me is a force of compassion and hope. I used to think God was against me and now I think God has been fighting for me all along. You know when that massacre happened at Dunblane and the bishop said, 'God's heart is the first to break.' Well, I used to think God did things to you to screw your bloody life up basically.

I know that was a completely warped view of God and that God's heart is the first heart to break when people suffer. I'm aware of that for the blokes at work when I'm praying for them getting off the drink and finding it so difficult. I feel uncondemned now. I mean I haven't been condemned all along but it never felt like that. Sometimes I'm looking for a feeling when I'm praying. I've tried to stop doing that because you don't always get a feeling. The feeling is a gift and it comes out of the blue. I once read a book called *Embracing the Light* by Betty Edie. It's an absolutely wonderful book and it's her experiences of when she died and was resuscitated. She talks about there being 'large, bright prayers' that reach from earth to heaven and the angels are waiting to answer.

When we do our prayer times, I try not to do them in a floppy way but to put myself in behind them. Our previous Minister General had cancer and she got secondaries, and we heard that she might not live till February. It was Christmas and I prayed and prayed. I thought, you know you are supposed to pray for God's will. Well, I said, 'Sod God's will, cure her, make her better. She is such a wonderful force of good in the world, I don't want that to be taken away.' And I prayed bright large prayers like it said in this book, and I wasn't the only person doing that. And on her last visit to the hospital they said 'We can't understand it but we can't see the cancer'. That just thrills me to bits, I find that elating.

I think now about all the times I have pleaded with God to help me. I never thought I was being helped because I wanted it instantly. When I look back, I can see that God hasn't rejected me, and I don't believe she rejects anybody. When there is suffering, I think the bishop is right that God's is the first heart to break. You can never prove it, but I always think that if all the people in the world stopped praying, there'd be a huge difference in the world. A huge negative difference. I can never prove that but that's what I believe. My father will ask me about suffering and, before I can answer, he'll say, 'Don't say to me "God works in mysterious ways".' And he's asking me to explain the mind of God. And I'll say that I don't know, I haven't got a clue why that has happened to that person, but I still believe there is a God of compassion and love. And he says 'Prove it', but I can't prove it. I don't have to prove it. I know it.

If I try to compare it to other things like a court of law they could say; 'Where's the evidence?' And there might not be evidence. It might be just something, say, about a person, that you know by an instinct inside you. If you can't prove it, that doesn't mean it's not true. When I met this bloke who ran the hostel, I said to him, 'Prove to me there is a God' and he said, 'My life is the proof.' And he was right, because he loved us. He loved us without wanting anything from us. He was the opposite of a dirty old man. I was nineteen and he was fifty-two but there was nothing like that in it. He just loved you. It was the love of Christ. So when he said that, I thought, 'Yes. Your life is proof of it, darling.'

In the last three years, my relationship with God has deepened the way it would with another person. Now I spend time with God like I would with my best friend. I make myself a cup of coffee and make myself comfortable; I can be slumped and pray if I like. I used to think it was more spiritual to be upright. Now I don't mind if I drift in and out of sleep and pray. God is with you anyway, she's just waiting for you to tune in there. If I pray for two minutes out of every ten that I sit there, then that is a good day, but that's what I judge as prayer – the other eight might also be prayer.

I've learnt now that I'm not worthless. I know that I'm loved by God and I'm somebody. That has happened to me in three years. My love of God has grown back, not that I could tell it in a theological way but in a 'feeling and knowing it in my heart' way. Before I came here, I'd pray when it suited me if I was in the mood. Mostly I wasn't in the mood. Here it's part of the life and, if you've said you're going to live this life, you do it. Not that anyone's going to check whether you do it or not but, if you're going to take the life seriously, then you need to do what is part of your commitment. That constant sticking at something makes that thing shift.

Like I said, I've stopped looking for the feeling in it. I always knew there was a God once I'd met her the first time, but I couldn't believe she loved me. But I know now. I see it with people on the streets. They are broken. They have been so damaged by the rejection. That's why they are drinking. Because they can't hold the level of rejection inside. They think they are worthless but I know in myself as I'm praying for them that God is bleeding over them, not condemning them. They think they are worthless, as if alcoholism was some kind of moral defect instead of an illness.

God speaks to me through my emotions. That's the kind of person I am. She can find any way of speaking to you that is the best way for you. I can be stabbed by a line of something, almost like a physical feeling that tells me about God. For example, there is a line that we say in the morning prayer that goes,

> In the tender compassion of our God
> The dawn from on high shall break upon us.

That breaks over me like a wave. And there was another thing I read, and God spoke to me in this as well, Murray Bodo's book *The Song of the Sparrow*. He was talking about God and he says, 'He applauds when all other hands are still and when my own heart doubts my worth.' And to me, that was God speaking to me off the page. I wanted to stop people in the street and say, 'Did you know that God applauds when all other hands are still and when your own heart doubts your worth?' I could have stopped people and said it. I could have got a balloon and hung it from the bloody sky.

On this mission we went into this school and I thought, 'What do I want them to get out of this?' and I thought I wanted them to know that God knows their name and that they are worth everything.

Sometimes I pray for knowledge of God and wait and see what

happens. I always want something specific to happen and it doesn't very often, but something might happen in the week and I think, 'Oh Yeah'. Like I got caught up in the Brixton riots. I was trying to get home through the town. I didn't know it was the riots. I just knew it was a hell of a funny turn-out. There was a funny silence and I thought it didn't feel right. There was these blokes in white masks and suddenly the riot police came down and all hell broke loose. There was cars being burnt, gun shots, shouting and throwing things. I'd never been so frightened in all my life. It was the white masks on black guys that frightened me. I got home OK, but I became frightened of young black guys on the buses. I hated that. I felt I suddenly had prejudices and I was a mass of all the things I hated. I didn't want to be like that. Anyway, I prayed about this and I joined this counselling course and two-thirds of the people on it were black – and there was quite a few young black guys, and that cured me. And I think that is how God deals with things. Sometimes he speaks to you directly and sometimes it's through situations. I didn't want to be stuck with prejudice, and I'm not stuck with it now.

As a novice, you're deciding if this is the place where you are meant to take vows or not. But it's not just me; it's the other people. You've got to be liveable with to be in community. It has to feel right to other people and not just to you. I'm pretty sure I should be here, and the feedback I've had from other sisters says the same. Sometimes you just know something's right.

Father John, the bloke who runs where I work, he's a man of vision. There ain't many people like him, and, when you're talking, he'll come up with something that is way beyond what's being said. He's a visionary. And I know that's God speaking through him. I've learnt a lot about God through him, God's attitude to people, because what I've learnt there is that she never gives up on people. This bloke never gives up on anyone. No matter how many times they go out back on the streets drunk again and come back to detox, he never gives up.

I'm seeing God in person there, not the whole of God, but one of God's attributes.

If someone says, 'Well God doesn't answer my prayers', I say, 'How do you know – unless you put a timer on it?' Or I say, 'You might be praying for something that might not be for your benefit or you might be asking the wrong questions.'

You know when that pope died? I forget his name. They are all called John something or other. He'd only been pope for a couple of weeks. Someone asked Cardinal Hume what he thought God's will was in that and he said he didn't have a clue. And I laughed and I thought, 'Thank God he's honest.' I've had plenty that's been unanswered. I'm not all for God because I feel I'm always answered, but I can see, looking back, that some things I thought would have been just right would have been wrong for me. So you have to wait.

Sometimes I think that God only uses human beings to force her way down here in some way. Like, if you look at the problem of people starving which is an obvious one, you have to alter the hearts of people to get anything to happen. Like the homeless, they never do anyone any harm but the way people treat them you wouldn't believe it. By changing yourself a lot of prayers can be answered.

Like if I'm praying for a homeless alcoholic, I have to work on my attitude. I mustn't be frightened, if I'm talking to someone, that I might get lice or nits or something. I have to build up a relationship in order for prayers to be answered. People have to be treated with great respect. And God can't answer every prayer without changing the whole of nature. If someone's wife has died and they say, 'I prayed to God to keep her alive and my prayers weren't answered' – but it's not the person who has died, because I do believe they are in a much better place, but the one who's left that suffers; maybe it can alter them in some way for good. I don't know. I don't have God's vision.

Poverty, Chastity and Obedience

Poverty. Well I got the house I wanted and I got the car. It's almost like I had to have everything that I thought would make my life great. Well, fine. They were nice. I enjoyed them but they weren't anything deep.

When I travelled to join the community the car held three of us and everything I owned. And with three of us there wasn't a lot of room. In the end I'd like to get my belongings down to two suitcases because I've still got extra stuff I don't need. I like the idea of freeing yourself of things. Someone said, if you have a possession and you value it as it deserves and give it time and space, then keep it. But once you've ceased to notice it, let it go. And I like that. The process of freeing myself of things goes on.

As regards money, there is a box here and you can take what you need for fares and that. Obviously you think very carefully before spending any money that belongs to everyone. The thing I miss is trashy magazines, but it forces me to read books – which I really love anyway. At the moment I'm reading *Fat Girl Dancing with Rocks*, and I've just read Sara Maitland's *Daughter of Jerusalem* and *Three Times Table*. I don't do spiritual reading every day. I do it sometimes and then I wait a while until something else takes my fancy.

I miss having the TV to myself. It's not the same with other people watching it. I used to watch documentaries, *Casualty* and the soaps. I used to watch all the soaps – even *Neighbours* – and I loved being able to get videos. We do watch TV, but here you can be halfway through a film and someone will come in and tell you they've had a bad journey – and you're sitting watching someone having their leg cut off or something.

Poverty? We don't experience poverty like people who are homeless.

★ ★ ★

Chastity. I've had sexual relationships but I've never slept around. I miss sex. I stopped having it eighteen months before I joined. I went celibate before I entered, because I was really serious about joining. I wish I'd known that the last time was going to be the last time. Sometimes I feel fine about it, and other times I think that I can't believe I'll never have sex again. If I say the words 'for the rest of my life', that is too big a thing to say. But that is what I believe because I wouldn't break my vows. If I really had to have sex, I'd have to leave.

I'm not in a relationship with anyone and I wouldn't have sex outside a relationship. If a relationship formed while I was working with someone, I'd have to rethink whether I'm supposed to be in community, but I don't think it will, because I'm meant to be here. I miss sex and I'm glad I enjoyed it. When I entered the other convent when I was twenty-two, I hadn't had sex before I went in, and I felt a bit of a fraud because I had nothing to give up. But it means more to me now, because I've got some choice. To choose to be celibate when you've got choice is very different. Just because I was single before I come in doesn't mean I was celibate. A lot of church people like to assume you are celibate if you are single. Well, that's their problem if they think that. I don't assume anything like that and it's none of my business.

I used to think, 'Who are these married Christian people to think that not only have I not got a partner living at home but I can't have sex, either?' I never ever felt that I cheapened myself in any way by having sex. I think that sex is there to be enjoyed. I call an orgasm 'zinging' because your whole body would zing. And I think that's great. I love a God who can design a body that zings when you have sex. That is an amazing gift to give people.

I've chosen to be celibate because you can't have community life and a special relationship – and I've chosen this. But outside community, if someone's in a happy sexual relationship I think 'Good for you, darling.'

And kids. I used to think, 'Do I want a child or do I just want the experience of motherhood?' I used to wonder what my baby would have looked like. For about two years I had what I'd have called a 'pram ache', and then that subsided. I knew I couldn't have lots of other experiences if I had this one. When I taught in a classroom and I asked them what they wanted to do with their lives they'd say, 'Get married, and have a baby' and I'd say, 'That's fine, but have you looked at other alternative ways of life?' I've chosen not to have kids and I feel that's the right choice for me.

★ ★ ★

Obedience. Well, here people don't tell you to do petty things you don't want to do. We all work at doing things for the common good – like you would with anyone you are living with, for the good of others and yourself. That's the way we run our houses.

The thing I find difficult is the big things – like the fact I've got to go to Newcastle-under-Lyme. I love it here in Brixton and I'm afraid I might not be as happy there. I don't mind the little things like getting up at 6.30 a.m. when I'd rather lie in bed. I don't mind the little things. It's the big things. I've been very happy here and I hope it works out there. I've enrolled for O level Islamic studies, the culture and the religion, because I'm interested in that, and I thought I'd meet people with interests beyond their immediate environment. That's an example of being positive about something I'd really rather not do. If it was completely up to me, I'd stay here.

I call God 'she' because I need to get away from this male imagery stuff. The Church in general gets on my nerves like that. It's quite different. It's not so much that I'm thinking of God as a mother because I don't think of God as a father, but more to think of the feminine side of God. When I think of God as female, there is a totally different feel because I think of women as more intuitive. I'm generalising, I don't care if I am. I think of them as more intuitive, more compassionate and less aggressive. There is a lot of male imagery in the Bible – the armour of God and all that. It doesn't speak to me at all. I like to think of God in a softer sort of way. That doesn't mean God isn't challenging.

But challenging without all the male crap that goes with it.

If I say 'she' in my mind, that gives me an entry and a closeness to God that I can't get when I say 'he'.

Living in community with other people is challenging. There are people here, who, if I'd met outside, we'd never have spoken two words. Here you get to know people at a very deep level. When I joined the convent, there was someone I didn't get on with at all; there was a lot of friction. Because we were having to live together, you can't say, 'Oh stuff it' and ignore them. So we talked it out and it was very painful for both of us. We decided we didn't want to give each other a wide berth. We really wanted to go for something better and it's really turned out to be something good. There is a huge bonus in working through things. I find it very exciting working out relationships. It's like the overcoming of war in a little way. There is something easy about living alone. This is harder but it's very enriching.

I have freedom here that I've never had before. I felt I had to compete financially, that I was judged on what I could earn or what I wore, or whether I drove a decent car. Those things are all completely meaningless. Here, when we have to shop for clothes, we go to second-hand shops and I love that. I'm earning £5,000 a year but it doesn't matter because the money all goes in a common fund anyway. So money ceases to be very relevant. It doesn't matter if one person's earning and one person isn't. In some way I felt I had to compete before. I never want to work anywhere again where I have to get smart and try and make an impression by the way I look.

The other thing I like about community is that it allows people to change. If there is someone who has been really difficult to live with or whatever, you'll hear people say, 'Oh, they've changed. They're not like that any more.' They don't put a label on people and make them stay there. People go for growth and healing and I find that brilliant. I want to be part of a community that does that. In community you realise how desperately sick and in need of healing people are.

Community is only a cross-section of society. I don't think they are any more or less sick than anyone else. I don't think any Christians are any more or less healed than anyone else, because God starts healing from where people are. If you look at community, you think 'What an odd bunch' – but it works, because the one thing you have in common is God, and there is a hope in it that I'd like to see everywhere. That doesn't mean all my relationships in community are right. There are some people that I can't hardly get on with at all but I don't think that's that. It's only for now – they'll change and so will I.

The prayer life here is like the sea. It goes on and on and it's wonderful to be part of that. I've always been spiritually ambitious in terms of wanting to know God more and have more understanding of things. And the way the life is here is a privilege spiritually. I'm going to travel more spiritually in terms of wisdom and getting closer to God . . . well, it would take me ten years outside to travel what I've done here in three.

People say, 'You're giving a lot up', and part of me would like to say, 'Oh, yes, it's a very sacrificial life'. But, if it's what you want to do, whatever you are doing, it's not a sacrificial life. I don't find it harder than any other way of life. It's different. And, if it's what you're meant to be doing, it's a good way of life.

Since this interview, Rose left Brixton to spend some time at the Newcastle-under-Lyme house of the community. There she took a course of training with the Samaritans and was asked to lead prayer days and 'quiet days', which she said was 'far too quiet'. Now she's back in her beloved Brixton and has taken her first vows. Rose works in a local psychiatric hospital helping ex-patients find work and as a volunteer for the Kairos community (residential care for homeless alcoholics who wish to detox).

She says: 'I've started playing the viola and joined a late starters' orchestra. It's wonderful. And I'm doing a bungee jump to raise money for the Kairos Community. Put that in the book because then they'll know I'm brave, won't they? One of the sisters said they'll have to sponsor her just to look.'

Rose is still hoping to be invited for tea at Lambeth Palace one day to meet the Archbishop. I said I thought she should become the Archbishop.

sister esther

*As my dear niece said 'Wasn't it enough when you were
in the ecumenical community in Germany and wearing
that dowdy old pinafore-dress? Now you are getting up at
four-thirty in the morning and living in an English
community with a load of old monks!'*

sister esther

COMMUNITY OF THE SERVANTS OF THE WILL OF GOD

MONASTERY OF CHRIST THE SAVIOUR

HOVE, SUSSEX, ENGLAND

The air in Brighton and Hove has a sweetness well-matched to a sunny afternoon in the garden at this little monastery. When you visit, the door is opened by Brother Mark, who, at eighty, has a wisdom and serenity that most of us would take one hundred and eighty years to acquire. He might have married Romeo and Juliet against their parents' wishes, he has that kind of twinkle in his eye.

The upstairs front room of the terraced house is the chapel, where the walls are covered with extraordinary paintings of scenes from Creation to Revelation. Here the four brothers and two sisters use a form of service which they have developed themselves, drawing on the ancient Orthodox forms of prayer and praise.

Sister Esther looks like a teenager amongst them. Her hair, clearly visible with her informal veil, is jet black without a touch of grey and she has a huge and welcoming smile across the chapel. I am amazed to learn that she is fifty-four years old, making her the oldest of the novices I interviewed.

After a formal lunch in the tiny refectory, Esther suggests that we enjoy the garden. The sea-gulls kept us company and occasionally threatened to drown out the soft-spoken German sister. Speaking English so clearly was hard for Esther and she altered the interview extensively after seeing it in print, to clarify each phrase. Her vulnerability, sensitivity and honesty shine.

It all began with a vision I had. I'm not sure whether I was awake or asleep. It was in the early hours of the morning but it didn't feel like a dream. It seemed as though I was standing at the edge of a lake and beside me was a young boy. We were looking at the rising sun which became larger and larger. We both were fascinated by the beauty and suddenly I heard the boy exclaiming 'The glory of God!' over and over again. Then I was no longer conscious of the boy's presence. I continued to look at the light and I was drawn more and more into the brightness, although one can't normally do that without being blinded. Together with this drawing was a feeling of utter holiness. Inside the light, I became aware of a figure with black hair and a long white garment, bowing down repeatedly towards the very centre of the sun. I was moved to tears. I wondered if the figure represented Christ, but later I thought that if the light were like God then Christ would be part of that light. So I wondered if the figure represented a human being – or even myself?

Then there followed a series of different pictures. The first I saw was a sunny seashore followed by a landscape which I realised was not from my own country, but another place, although it did resemble my native Germany. And the last picture – still in my imagination – was a particular scene in a wooded countryside sloping down to a small valley. I saw shadowy figures walking about slowly in ones and twos on the top of the hill. It was rather like looking through a mist, or the light of the very early dawn.

I trained as a deaconess in the Lutheran Church in South Germany and I also belonged to an active ecumenical community (founded in the early sixties) that includes families as well as individual brothers and sisters. We had branches in various places and so I was able to work in Switzerland and Berlin as well as other parts of Germany. It was a truly fulfilling life and I enjoyed doing all the usual work in parishes: youth work, running holiday camps, teaching, counselling, visiting the sick and the elderly, helping the life of the Church and the local community in any and all the ways that were needed.

In all this I never forgot my 'vision' of twelve years ago and eventually I reached a stage in my spiritual life where I was drawn to ask God more seriously about its meaning. Almost without my realising it, my prayer had deepened as a result of having this experience. I gradually discerned the need for a greater prayer life in our church and so I started to create more prayer groups in my parish. I was drawn to learn about the mystical side of faith and its rich tradition in the Christian Church. I didn't then know any religious communities within the Lutheran tradition in Germany that were dedicated to the contemplative lifestyle.

During a sabbatical period I asked an expert in this field and discovered that England has a number of contemplative communities inside the Anglican Church. I was forty-seven and I had no family or friends in England, and I had only the sort of English you learn as a tourist – 'Good morning, can you tell me the direction of the railway station, please?' I felt that in order to find out more about the contemplative tradition I would need to come to Britain. I think it was what would be called an act of blind faith.

I had planned to visit the community of the Sisters of the Love of God in Oxford (the community from which you have interviewed Sister Judith), but first I looked for an intensive English course of three months, and so it happened that I came to Hove, next to Brighton, in Sussex. The language school had arranged accommodation for me with a family and I started my course. I never knew that learning a language could be so difficult and take so long. But really I did enjoy it.

Just after the end of the course I spent a holiday with the Oxford sisters and took for my reading the lectures *Increase of Prayer* by Father Gilbert Shaw. O God, what a revealing reading this was and now I'm busy translating it into German.

One Bank Holiday I decided to look at some of the churches in Hove and found St Patrick's Church practically next to my lodgings, its door invitingly open. I went in and saw an attractive church in an Anglo-Catholic style. To my surprise my favourite Trinity icon was hanging above a central altar. The pews had been moved from their original position and arranged in a circle. It was beautiful and reminded me very much of my community's chapel. There was evening prayer followed by a Communion service every evening, finishing about 8 o'clock. This suited me very well between my day of study and my evening homework. So I started to attend the services religiously! I was particularly impressed with the ministry of this church, with its work among the homeless. They run an overnight shelter for homeless men in a part of the church and they manage to get a good number of them re-housed.

I was surprised to see several monks present at the services in St Patrick's. It turned out that in the same street as the church was a community of contemplative monks. They invited me to take lunch with them and I told them why I had come to England and of my struggles to learn English. They asked if I might like to consider going for a weekend to visit the main monastery of their community in Crawley Down in West Sussex. A German monk happened to be staying with them at that time, so I was delighted to accept the invitation. What a relief to be able to talk to someone in German about the spiritual life there.

This community, the Servants of the Will of God, is rediscovering a tradition which existed before the Church split up to form the Eastern and the Western Churches in the eleventh century. Their services draw on and make use of both traditions. I found that the services include a lot of bowing followed by silent prayer and it was then that I suddenly remembered the opening part of my vision.

The monastery in Crawley Down is set in woodland with a small farm attached. One day as I was walking around I was suddenly astonished. Surely this was the very view that I had seen five years ago in the early hours of the morning when I was in Berlin. Yet here I was, in the grounds of an English monastery. It was all quite overwhelming. 'Oh God,' I asked, 'what does this mean?'

So that is how I ended up going to the Superior and telling him my story. Could I join the monks? He looked surprised at first, but he showed great understanding and was prepared to accept that I might have a real call. At that time there was no question of any sisters in the community. However eventually I became the first woman 'Seeker' in the Hove monastery. A 'Seeker' is a lay person who is trying out a vocation to the monastic life, and I did this while still going to the language school around the corner. At that time there were ten fully professed monks altogether. Now there are three more brothers and, as well as myself, two other sisters. And I still live up the street from that church I discovered.

I'm continually very surprised at the way God has brought me here – but perhaps that applies to all of us! In the meantime God is leading us on to grow in the spiritual life of prayer – and this is quite challenging enough for now.

In thinking back to my childhood I realise that I was much loved, being the youngest, and the only daughter of the family. But I was born into a very troubled time of war and we spent many long hours huddled in the cellar. It was an extraordinary mixture of daily life, work and war. Perhaps I should explain that my father had refused to join the denunciation of Jewish people and he was regarded with suspicion by Nazi sympathisers among his fellow town-councillors. So much so that our house was marked: 'Friend of the Jews'.

Also I remember the house being used as a temporary YMCA. We put up various refugees and we also housed long-term evacuees. When we found it all too much my father comforted us by saying: 'Remember, with each stranger we are sheltering an angel!' And my mother did whatever was in her strength. We were very lucky, we never went hungry and we were able to give to others. And often in the evening my mother would play the piano delightfully and we all joined in with voices or with other instruments – forgetting the troubles of those times. On Sundays, after church, friends, neighbours and relations came to our house and recounted things that had happened to them during the week; sometimes we even discussed the week's sermon with a glass of wine or home-made liqueur.

Once school started we children still had our part to play by helping in the house and garden or on the farm. It was hard work then but my father saw to it that we also had plenty of fun. I remember one of my special harvest tasks after getting home from school was to bring fresh drink and food to the field where everyone was already looking out for me to enjoy a drink and a rest in the shade of a tree.

By the time I was sixteen there was a change in the family set-up. My older brother took over the management of one of our two farms which had previously been rented out and I was asked to take on the domestic side of things for the time being. He was young and energetic. We naturally had great plans for developing the whole farm, including designing a new house and farm buildings.

One summer day when I was nineteen, I was seriously injured in an accident with one of our horse-drawn farm machines. It gave me a very strong experience of how fragile our life is and that God can take it any time. While I lay recovering I wondered what God's plan for me might be and I offered the life he had given me back for his service.

This is why I went to a Bible school for two years and then to theological college at twenty-five. At that time a relationship had grown up with a young man who was training to be a pastor. I was very much in love, and he loved me. Of course, we were not members of a church that required celibacy and we could have got married, and I could have still gone to theological college and he have been a pastor, but somehow that was not to happen.

One day I felt an unexpected change in him, but I said nothing. And then I had a curious experience, as though a hand had come between us and suddenly all the feeling I had for him was taken away. I couldn't stop crying and he was bewildered. When I told him how I felt, he was open and admitted having a similar experience. And this led us both to ask again what the right way was for us. Perhaps it is good to have been in love before you enter any community because then you understand what you are giving up.

We decided to wait for a year and hope that God would reveal more of his plans for us. If I was going to enter a religious community I would need to have a feeling of real joy about it. Without joy I would not be able to embrace this kind of life wholeheartedly. So I boldly asked God to send me that joy if he really wanted this of me. And joy filled me.

We are not puppets. We are 'made in the image of God'. And he is waiting to give us his love if we will accept it. We are all more or less in trouble because we have lost our relationship with God. As it is, we have been given total freedom, and in it we are often like over-active children running around not listening to our parents, and so we are dissatisfied and unhappy.

It seems as though we are all searching, and we are each making up our own idea of God to suit ourselves. But it doesn't work and we simply need to say 'I was wrong, I walked away from you instead of walking with you.' For me the contemplative life is an attempt to rediscover this true relationship, on behalf of us all, and to walk with God in joy.

Poverty, Celibacy and Obedience

Poverty. I no longer see this primarily from the material side. I took these vows when I was twenty-nine and at that age it was not easy for me because our family was comfortably off, we enjoyed beautiful surroundings, owned our own horses and had a good lifestyle and great hospitality. I really couldn't imagine how difficult it is to lose your home and all material things. I didn't know how much my soul clung to these things. On the one side there is enormous freedom to give things away and live in faith, but you realise how quickly you are ready to cling to 'things' again. Now I am looking at the vows freshly, it is easier for me to be without possessions because God has given me something richer, which is an inner life of prayer. In the prayer life you are totally stripped of outside things. This is the normal understanding of poverty, but there is something much deeper – poverty and humility of spirit, in order to find true freedom in God. I think it is essential to live a more enclosed life for the first few years so that you can experience this stripping and find a will for it, so as to find God inside you. You need to find and know God not only in nature and outside yourself but inside yourself as well. You suddenly realise that your inner life can be very rich. I'm not saying that it is necessary for every Christian to give up everything, but for those seeking the contemplative life one needs to get rid of possessions in order to be free for others and live in God's will. I still have a bank account, though I make no use of it, and I'll have that till I take the final vows.

To give up everything you own really is to gain more and to see that God is working inside you and using all your abilities, no longer for your own benefit but for his glory. There are enormous riches but you have to have faith. To walk in faith for life is a very hard process but not without delight, or seeing glimpses of heaven. It is encouraged through every single act of faith. If you endure, you reach depths and then suddenly there is a change, suddenly a new freedom comes and you see life differently and you no longer cling to material things. You don't have to possess things, and those which you use you can enjoy in a detached way as a gift of God.

★ ★ ★

Celibacy. This is hard. As natural creatures we tend to be against celibacy. But there is a way through contemplation that God becomes your total fulfilment. This comes as a surprise, but is the actual life of your soul at the very point where God meets you. The contemplative life leads you inside and makes you aware that next to your sexuality, deeper than your sexuality, is a life going on which is the spiritual life. You have to go deeper than your sexuality and this is only possible if you give all these depths of yourself to God and allow him to work within you. It is as though you were digging up treasures you never knew were there. But the digging can be very painful and disturbing because it reveals you to yourself. Perhaps you are even shocked, lost or frightened as if you were falling into a pit and you pray: 'My God, help me!' And then there emerges a richness, not of emotional feelings, although there are emotions too, but a total fulfilment where the soul is filled with the riches of God's grace.

That does not mean that it is essential to be celibate in order to experience this, but if you are not celibate you may have more difficulty because you have to give yourself so totally to God to learn fully that there is no greater treasure. It is dependent on total giving to God, total awareness that God is all in your life. You long for God to enrich your life and then you have to wait for him. And there is, at the same time, a stripping of your own nature and your passions, not to diminish you in any way but in order that you may find the core of your spiritual life. Like the description Christ gives of 'living water'. It is a spring that you find in yourself which he develops. To find this is the search of the contemplatives, and it's worth spending your whole life on this. There are many witnesses who have found this 'living spring' and who have written about it – Teresa of Avila or John of the Cross as well as many others who have followed through the centuries. This living water is a gift we all can receive if we are faithful to God our creator.

In my early thirties I was grateful that we were not just women but were brothers and sisters in the community and I think men and women are dependent on each other for our whole development. We had shared meals and shared services till we were able to build separate houses for the brothers and sisters. Our common aim was to pursue a spiritual life that would not involve being drawn into marriage but to be available for the Church, for other people and for the world. But I was glad the brothers were there and I was glad that I had fallen in love earlier in life.

Our celibate witness supported the families somehow as well. I remember them saying things to us like: 'Through seeing the life of you brothers and sisters we can see that to love Jesus Christ is enough.'

I remember a woman teacher at the Bible school telling us – we were all in our twenties – saying to us that if we felt God was calling us to a total giving to him by joining a community, then we should try to fall in love first, so as to understand what we were giving up! And today I would add – also to be more able to be enriched by God's grace.

It is a great pity that sex and love are quite often confused with each other. To have sex so early when you are so young can't compare with the richness of the experience if you are in love and have the right circumstances around you. Although people do not always see it, God will guide each one, as a loving friend, to the beauties of life. And even if people have had bad experiences and broken relationships, Paul does say that all things come together for good if you believe. And there is always the God-given way of repentance and a fresh start.

It is important not to deny or suppress your sexuality but to offer all of yourself to God so that he can show you how to use your sexual energy in other ways. If you fall in love with God and offer all your feelings, God does respond. It is true that there is a time, maybe years, when there is a strain and you wonder how you can offer all of your sexuality to God, but God has created you as a sexual being and you can't offer your mind to God and not include your body. I think it's good to be as natural as possible before God in your private prayer – using your whole body, bowing, kneeling and so on. And when you love God over all, he does fill your heart with an amazing joy.

In my work I was always surrounded by children and I took much joy in their natural love, so freely expressed. But there was a time when I was working in an area with many young families, when I found the fact that I was never to have children very difficult. I brought all this willingly to God in prayer and asked that he would make me fruitful in another way, as is promised in the gospel. When we pray we don't have to suppress our feelings, but to open ourselves completely to God and then he is able to fill us. Does all this sound very strange? I can only say there is a costly pearl, not easily found, which makes the struggle worth while.

★ ★ ★

Obedience. The first obedience is always to God. But it is important that you have a good guide along the way. The leaders of this community are very gentle in their guidance of any individual and the way that they interpret God's leading. And they are men of love, really they have God's love in them. They have found these depths that I was speaking of earlier where the love of Christ can develop in you and enrich your whole nature. You know this when you meet them, that they have a special gift from God to lead people in a loving way. They know the difficulties and battles we have to get rid of our desire to secure what we ourselves want, which is not always the deepest way that God may want for us. The way of obedience, I found, is only fruitful if obedience is given in love. For the first years this can be very difficult because we are by nature all rebellious and proud and want to be in control of our own lives.

My aim in coming to England was to find out where God was leading me. I only knew that I wanted to learn about the life of contemplation. I had no idea what this life was really about – all I knew was that you had more time for prayer. It's very different from that. It's true that you do have more time for prayer, but it changes you totally in your thinking and your understanding and your being. The change is a suffering in many ways, to discover your true self, so as to 'become prayer' as Father Gilbert Shaw would say. The caterpillar has to become a butterfly, to quote the example given by St Teresa of Avila.

But back to obedience. I think obedience is not only for an individual to obey someone in a special case, but also to listen together to the voice or plan of God and the leading of the Holy Spirit. Very often we don't have patience to listen, which is sad. To be able to act in a mature response in the way of obedience in small matters is a sign of great humility and love. Every small step helps us on the way – but not without falling, falling again, and getting up again.

I found that it meant going on in complete faith. All familiar things and people were taken away – even my own language – and I had to start again from scratch like a child starting school; only, I was a child of forty-seven. I never knew what hard work and humiliation it would be to learn to communicate in any detail in another language. For me the daily reading time always meant hard study, to understand the high-flown language of the mystical writers and to master a new vocabulary. I came here where nobody knew me or my background and I couldn't even express myself properly. I just lived and trusted God. It was a way of total faith. In times of decisions God has encouraged me with sayings of Abraham, like; 'Stay in this land and I will be with you and bless you.' Or, 'So Abraham left as the Lord had told him.'

Even now, I still don't fully understand God's continuing purpose for me within the contemplative life. So it has all been a huge lesson in obedience and trusting God. It has felt as if God has led me, even in small details like finding the right book to read or helping me to get up so early – which is by no means a small detail. Yes, it's a paradox – there is a deep certainty and yet you see nothing. It's a bit like walking in a valley between high mountains, when you can't see the view but you know that it is there.

I know God is there because I feel within me the certainty of his presence. God is like a partner who lives next to you and in you. You are in him and he is in you. Sometimes God just reveals his presence and sometimes he actively tests you and challenges you and it seems to me the more you trust him the more he challenges you again and again, so that you may grow in spirit and in love.

God uses a rich variety of approaches to win our attention and to use our abilities too. Even here where we sit in the garden, the tiny details of the flowers show a little of his glory. Yes, the whole creation is designed by God, simply to give us pleasure in his greatness, wisdom, love and omnipotence. There is nothing in us, too, which he can't change, enrich, develop and make beautiful provided we open up ourselves fully without holding back.

Another way I experience God is in silence, as when we look at the calm sea and recollect our thoughts, which tend to buzz around like a swarm of bees. It's best not to try to capture them, but to offer them to God and then wait till they become prayer. So I wait upon God, in the expectation that his Spirit will silently grow. It may start with a deeper breathing and deeper rest bringing a true inner harmony and a feeling of the presence of God. His presence is deeper beyond our bodily knowledge or awareness. This is why we need time to get a glimpse of his presence. And this is also why we need much perseverance in offering our nature in repentance and accepting nothingness before God. This nothingness – far from being sheer horror – brings grace and freedom. God helps us to depend utterly on him and gives us a true realisation that we are part of his whole creation. It is then possible to understand the gospel in a deeper way so that it becomes real in all circumstances of life. Our sufferings are Christ's sufferings and his are ours. And our joy is a sharing in his resurrection. We long to love as he loves because we are aware of our own great lack of love. It seems to me that the only way of overcoming strife and hatred among people is to seek to increase love 'as Christ loved us'. True love. But it's a great adventure – to believe wholeheartedly that 'God is Love' and that he loves us only for love's sake and that nothing can separate us from that love. And here, I believe, is the ongoing invisible work of the contemplatives, whether they are inside or outside a monastery.

We have all learned how difficult it can be to achieve lasting inner peace. There seem to be such a lot of outward hindrances, like not having the right place, time or conditions. And then there are also the inner hindrances, as we all have our own strong will, our own opinions, our individual moods and so on which lead us to give up too easily. We may even feel that we are doing nothing and that the experience of silence is just a waste of time. But on the contrary, it is a precious gift of God which leads us to inward peace and therefore disperses all fear.

It is difficult today for people really to experience peace. So many people, even people who go to church or practise other spiritual disciplines, are afraid of silence. Some people always have the television or a radio on in their homes. We do not endure long enough to learn that we can experience God in this way of silence. We all need to learn to be at peace in silence, to find the peace in our hearts.

Esther has been at the Hove monastery with the brothers for six years.

The main Monastery of the community at Crawley Down in Sussex has a further nine brothers and now, one sister. One more brother has joined the community since this interview.

Sister Esther continues to renew her vows annually and will do so until she feels ready to take life vows.